AA

TOUR GUIDE
SCOTLAND

Produced by AA Publishing

Written by David Williams
Copy editor: Dilys Jones

Edited, designed, produced and
distributed by AA Publishing,
Fanum House, Basingstoke,
Hampshire RG21 2EA.

© The Automobile Association
1992

Maps © The Automobile
Association 1992

A CIP catalogue record for this book
is available from the British Library.

ISBN 0 7495 0431 5

Typesetting: Servis Filmsetting Ltd,
Manchester

Colour reproduction: Scantrans
P.T.E., Singapore

Printed and bound in Italy by
Printers S.R.L., Trento

The contents of this publication are
believed correct at the time of
printing. Nevertheless, the
publishers cannot accept
responsibility for errors or omissions,
or for changes in details given.

Every effort has been made to
ensure accuracy in this guide.
However, things do change and we
would welcome any information to
help keep the book up to date.

Published by AA Publishing

Cover picture: *Eilean Donan Castle*
Title page: *Red deer*
Right: *Scotland's Lion Rampant*

CONTENTS

INTRODUCTION

This book is not only a practical guide for the independent traveller, but is also invaluable for those who would like to know more about the country.

It is divided into 4 regions, each containing between 5 and 7 tours. The tours start and finish in the towns and cities which we consider to be the best centres for exploration. Each tour has details of the most interesting places to visit en route. Side panels cater for special interests and requirements and cover a range of categories – for those whose interest is in history, wildlife or walking, and those who have children. There are also panels which highlight scenic stretches of road along the route and which give details of special events, gastronomic specialities, crafts and customs. These are cross-referred back to the main text.

The simple route directions are accompanied by an easy-to-use map of the tour and there are addresses of local tourist information centres in some of the towns en route as well as in the start town.

Simple charts show how far it is from one town to the next in miles and kilometres. These can help you to decide where to take a break and stop overnight, for example. (All distances quoted are approximate.)

Before setting off it is advisable to check with the information centre at the start of the tour for recommendations on where to break your journey and for additional information on what to see and do, and when best to visit.

PUBLIC HOLIDAYS

The term 'Bank Holiday' has a restricted meaning in Scotland, where it does not necessarily signify a public national holiday.

Although Christmas Day and New Year's Day are generally accepted as national holidays, others vary throughout Scotland and are decided upon yearly by each region. For a comprehensive list of public holidays contact the Scottish Chambers of Commerce in Glasgow (*tel:* 041-204 2121) or, alternatively, contact the Scottish Tourist Board who will be able to supply the present year's remaining dates.

ENTRY REGULATIONS

Passports are required by all visitors including citizens of EC countries. Visas are not required for entry into Britain by American citizens, nationals of the British Commonwealth and most European countries.

CUSTOMS REGULATIONS

For goods bought outside the EC, you can import, duty free, 200 cigarettes or 100 cigarillos or 50 cigars or 250g of tobacco; one litre of alcohol over 22 per cent volume or 2 litres of alcohol not over 22 per cent volume or fortified or sparkling wine, plus 2 litres of still table wine; 50g of perfume and 9fl oz of toilet water. If goods are bought within the EC, you can import, duty paid, 300 cigarettes or 150 cigarillos or 75 cigars or 400g of tobacco; 1.5 litres of alcohol over 22 per cent volume or 3 litres of alcohol not over 22 per cent volume or fortified or sparkling wine, plus 5 litres of still table wine; 75g of perfume and 13fl oz of toilet water. However, you cannot have the duty free allowance as well as the duty paid EC allowance.

EMERGENCY TELEPHONE NUMBERS

Police, fire and ambulance *tel:* 999.

HEALTH

Inoculations are not required for entry to Britain. Health insurance is recommended for non-EC citizens.

CURRENCY

The unit of currency is the pound (£), divided into 100 pence. Coins are in denominations of 1, 2, 5, 10, 20 and 50 pence and one pound (£); Scottish notes are in denominations of £1, 5, 10, 20 and 50.

CREDIT CARDS

All major credit cards are widely accepted throughout Scotland.

BANKS

Banks are generally open between 09.30 and 15.30 hrs weekdays, though times do vary from bank to bank, and place to place. Some banks close for lunch.

POST OFFICES

Post Offices generally open from 09.00 to 17.30 hrs Monday to Friday and 09.00 to 12.00 hrs on Saturdays. Times and days may vary from place to place.

TIME

The official time is Greenwich Mean Time (GMT).

British Summer Time (BST) begins in late March when the clocks are put forward an hour. In late October, the clocks go back an hour to GMT. The official date is announced in the daily

Winter colours on the hills above Kilchurn Castle, Loch Awe

newspapers and is always at 02.00 hrs on a Sunday.

TELEPHONES

Insert coins after lifting the receiver; the dialing tone is a continuous tone.

Useful numbers:
Operator – 100
Directory Enquiries – 192
International Directory
    Enquiries – 153
International Operator – 155

TOURIST OFFICE

Scottish Tourist Board,
23 Ravelston Terrace,
Edinburgh EH4 3EU
tel: 031-332 2433.

ELECTRICITY

The standard electricity supply is 240 volts, 50 cycles AC. Plugs are three-pin. Shavers operate on 240 or 110 volts. Since most American appliances are designed to operate on 120 volts, 60 cycles, a transformer will be required. Visitors from Europe will also need an adaptor. Most hotels have special razor sockets which will take both voltages.

CONSULATES

Australia: Australian Consulate, Hobart House, 80 Hanover Street, Edinburgh *tel:* 031-226 6271.
Canada: Canadian Consul, 151 St Vincent Street, Glasgow G2 *tel:* 041-221 4415.
New Zealand: New Zealand High Commission, New Zealand House, Haymarket, London SW1 *tel:* 071-930 8422.
US: American Consulate General, 3 Regent Terrace, Edinburgh EH7 5BW *tel:* 031-556 8315.

To make an international call, dial 010 (the international code), then the country code, followed by the area code, omitting the first zero and the local number.

MOTORING
Documents
You must have a valid full driver's licence or an International Driving Permit. Non-EC nationals must have Green Card insurance.

Route directions
Throughout the book the following abbreviations are used for British roads:
M – motorways
A – main roads
B – local roads
unclassified roads – minor roads (unnumbered)

Breakdowns
Visitors who bring their cars to Britain and are members of a recognised automobile club may benefit from the services provided free of charge by the AA. The RAC also provides services.

Accidents
In the event of an accident, if the vehicle is fitted with hazard warning lights, they should be used. If available, a red triangle should be placed on the road at least 165 feet (50m) before the obstruction and on the same side of the road.

Speed limits
In built-up areas 30mph (48kph). Outside built-up areas 70mph

The white turbulent waters of the Falls of Dochart in autumnal spate above the lochside village of Killin

Trawling nets deck the harbour front at the tiny fishing village of Whitehills on the Moray Firth

(112kph) on motorways and dual carriageways; other roads 60mph (96kph). The above limits stand unless signposted otherwise.

Driving conditions
Driving is on the left.
Seatbelts are compulsory for drivers and all passengers, front and rear, if fitted.
Tolls are levied on certain bridges.
Roads in the highlands and islands of Scotland (and also in some country districts) are often narrow. On single track roads, pull into passing places only if they are on your left. Stop level with those on your right – the oncoming traffic will make the detour. Never hold up faster traffic approaching from behind, so stop at places to allow drivers to overtake.

Petrol
In the highlands, parts of Argyll and on the islands, petrol stations may close around 18.00 hrs and not all stations are open on Sundays.

Car hire and fly/drive
Drivers must hold a valid national licence or an International Driving Permit. The minimum age for hiring a car ranges from 18 to 25, depending on the model of car. With some companies, there is a maximum age limit of 70 years.
You can arrange to pick up your car in one town and return it in another. If you are going to hire a car, you can often get a good deal if you arrange a fly/drive package tour.

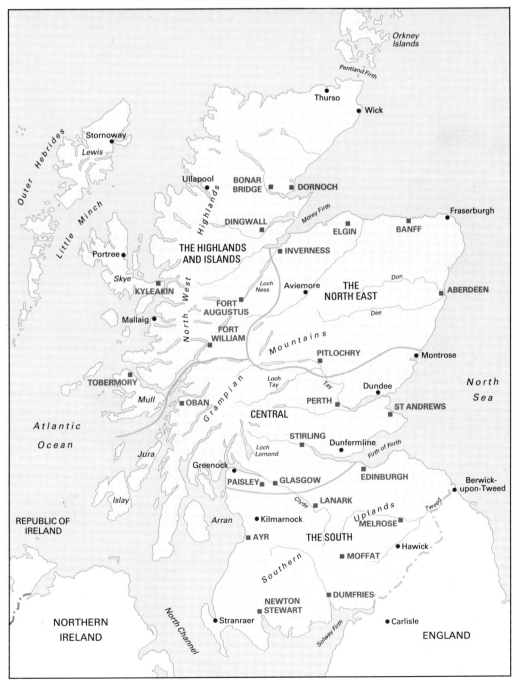

SOUTHERN SCOTLAND

Southern Scotland is dominated by the great mass of the Southern Uplands, the great band of hills which stretches right across the width of the country. For a long time it was easier to sail along the coastline than cross the hills, so the two coastal fringes were settled first. These narrow, fertile strips are still among the most populated parts of the region, with the best land devoted to cereals and herds of prime dairy cattle. Inland, the rolling uplands are home to the countless sheep which form the basis of the prosperous woollen and knitwear industries of the Borders.

The many castles and fortified houses found in the region are reminders of the centuries of border warfare that have shaped the history of the whole of southern Scotland. Cattle raiding, pillaging, looting and burning were almost commonplace, especially in the rich agricultural areas where the pickings were best. But perhaps the most poignant reminders of those turbulent days are the great Border abbeys of Melrose, Kelso, Jedburgh and Dryburgh which were mercilessly attacked again and again by the English. These magnificent buildings, with their wealth of splendid architectural detail, are like monuments to the art of wilful destruction. Fortunately, enough of their splendour survives to conjure the past

Today, the region is much more peaceful and most of today's 'invaders' come armed with a bucket and spade or a set of golf clubs. The eastern side of the country, with its beaches, seaside resorts, fishing villages and busy mill towns has been a tourist area for some time, with many of its best-known places made famous by the region's best publicist, Sir Walter Scott. The novelist and poet died worn out by debt and overwork, but his legacy of classic novels romanticizes the history and culture of the Scots people. The west coast's literary figure, Robert Burns, is highly regarded as 'a man of the people' and his special place in the Scots' heart can be judged by the number of memorials, plaques and statues that mark his journey through the country. All over the world, his birthday is celebrated on 26 January as Burns Night, a night of traditional Scots verse, song and a toast to the haggis!

The region can never match the grandeur of the western Highlands or the great museums and palaces of central Scotland, but it does offer a very relaxed way of life in an area imbued with traditions. Southern Scotland has never had the great factories of the central belt and its people are probably pleased with that fact. They are keen not to lose the unique flavour of their local culture and any visitor who witnesses a Border town's Common Riding, or rugby match, will soon learn how proudly independent the spirit is here.

Tour 1

The journey along the Clyde coast is one of the finest in this part of Scotland, with glorious views over the Firth of Clyde to Arran and the smaller islands of the Clyde. With such views, it is no wonder that many Scots retire to this area. For the visitor, this scenery provides the backdrop to many places associated with Robert Burns, the national poet and the Scots' favourite literary figure.

Tour 2

Many visitors bypass this corner of the country, but there is a wealth of picturesque villages, historic buildings, sandy beaches and many other attractions in this almost 'forgotten' land. The area is predominantly agricultural and the great absence of industry and big towns has meant that many antiquities have been preserved and older building styles have survived. This is one of the warmest and driest parts of Scotland, factors that have helped foster agriculture – and the palm trees!

Tour 3

The muddy creeks on the northern shore of the Solway Firth were havens to smugglers bringing contraband into Scotland. Given such a tradition, it comes as a surprise that the area's most famous figure was an exciseman – none other than Robert Burns, who spent his final years in the Dumfries area. The castles and granite towns of the coast contrast with the large forests and rolling farmland inland.

Tour 4

Although the Clyde is normally thought of as an industrial river, the upper reaches are thronged with orchards and market gardens. Add a few castles and an impressive canyon and the Clyde Valley soon becomes one of the most surprising areas in this part of Scotland. The moors and hills above the valley are no less interesting and they have been home to Iron Age people, Romans and farmers – and weekend gold prospectors!

John Rennie's granite bridge of 1813 spans the River Cree at Newton Stewart

Time outgraces the love that built Sweetheart Abbey. The foundress lies buried here with the heart of her husband

Tour 5

The tour follows many important river courses as they wind their way through the hills of the Southern Uplands, the land of the shepherd and the forester. Although the area's

population has never been large, it has certainly seen many visitors. Some were unwelcome as they came to raid and plunder; others, the early tourists, came to sample the peaceful countryside and the delights of two of the country's most southerly spas.

Tour 6

The name of Sir Walter Scott is writ large in this area. He lived and worked here and became one of Scotland's greatest novelists, to the extent that the *Waverley* novels gave their name both to a local railway line and to Edinburgh's main railway station. This is also the land of the ruins of the great Borders abbeys, impressive medieval buildings that stand as monuments to man's craftsmanship – and powers of destruction.

Tour 7

The Border Country, of which this is part, has long seen the coming and going of armies and the number of castles found here is a measure of how dangerous an area this once was. Much of the coastline is rugged, and the cliff scenery quite spectacular, though in the north of the region the coastal scenery becomes gentler, giving way to fine beaches and grassy links that are ideal for golf. Inland, the rich agricultural district of the Merse supports many pretty villages, most of which nestle under the shelter of the Lammermuirs.

1/2 days – 116 miles (187km)

THE LAND O' BURNS

Ayr ● Alloway ● Electric Brae ● Culzean Castle
Turnberry ● Kirkoswald ● Maybole ● Mauchline
Kilmarnock ● Irvine ● Largs ● Troon ● Ayr

Ayr is a traditional seaside resort, and its long sandy beach enjoys great popularity with locals and visitors alike. The town dates back to the 13th century and one of its most notable features is the *Auld Brig* which spans the River Ayr. Just downstream is the New Bridge, a relatively 'modern' structure that was erected in 1788 and rebuilt in 1878. The *Auld Kirk* (old church) of Ayr, which is near the Auld Brig, was built between 1654 and 1656 and was where the poet Robert Burns was baptised. The churchyard is worth exploring as it contains some elaborately carved headstones.

The fishing harbour is where the River Ayr meets the sea. This was once the chief port of western Scotland and it is still busy with fishing boats. *Ayr Castle*, built in 1197, was sited near here, but the tall walls seen today belong to the 17th-century citadel erected by Cromwell's forces. The town has three major parks, *Belleisle, Craigie* and *Rozelle*. Belleisle has a small zoo.

The hardy figure of a Highland cow in winter coat. The breed originated in the Scottish mountains, thriving on the poor conditions. Though usually yellowish in colour, they are sometimes black or red

---

ⓘ 39 Sandgate

> Take the **B7024** from Ayr for 3 miles (5km) to the village of Alloway.

Alloway, Strathclyde

1 The Land o' Burns Centre was established here as this was where the poet spent his early years. Robert Burns was born in 1759 and he is regarded not only as Scotland's national poet but as one of her greatest literary figures. Although lionized by the predominantly Edinburgh-based literary celebrities of his day, he never abandoned his roots in the west and continued to work as a small farmer, and later as an exciseman. Like many great artists, he was never fully appreciated until well after his death, but now there are hundreds of Burns Societies all over the world, each year celebrating the poet's birthday with such well-known favourites as *To a Haggis, Holy Willie's Prayer* and, probably his best-known work, *Auld Lang Syne.*

Opposite the Centre is the old ruined **kirk** where Burns' father is buried. This was a ruin even in Burns' day and it was here that Tam, in the poem *Tam o' Shanter,* saw warlocks, witches and Auld Nick (the devil).

The Burns Monument in Alloway, the birthplace in January 1759 of the celebrated Scottish poet. Spanning the River Doon is the Brig O' Doon of Tam O'Shanter fame, dating back perhaps to the 13th century

SPECIAL TO...

There are numerous celebrated golf courses along the Clyde Coast. The links along the coast are ideally suited to the game, and there are lots of bunkers! While most towns have courses, the best-known ones are at Troon, Ayr, Turnberry and Prestwick. They must surely rank as some of the most attractively sited courses in Britain.

Also nearby is the ancient and very beautiful **Auld Brig o' Doon** over which Tam escaped from the witches. Towering above the river is the **Burns Monument** which is set in a very pleasant park.

Burns was born in the little thatched cottage known the world over as **Burns Cottage**. His father, William Burnes, built it around 1730 and it has been well preserved, not only as a memorial to the poet, but as a good example of local village architecture of the time. This type of cottage is known as a 'but and ben', with the kitchen and living quarters at one end and the byre (cowshed) at the other. The neighbouring **museum** holds a vast amount of Burns memorabilia.

*Continue on the **B7024** for a short distance. Just after crossing the River Doon, turn right at an unclassified road to Doonfoot. Turn left when the coastal road (**A719**) is met, 8 miles (13km).*

Electric Brae, Strathclyde

2 After the A719 passes Dunure and turns inland at Culzean Bay, the road goes 'up' the Electric Brae, a well-known and mind-boggling optical illusion. A car might appear to be travelling downhill, but drivers who come to a halt will find the car rolling backwards! On a pleasant summer afternoon, there is sometimes quite a queue of cars on this stretch of road trying to roll 'uphill'. Take care!

*Continue on the **A719** for 5 miles (8km) to Culzean Castle.*

Culzean Castle, Strathclyde

3 The present building is based on a medieval tower house that was later developed as a massive country house set within extensive parkland.

It is now the National Trust for Scotland's major attraction and its **country park** has gardens, a nursery, a swan pond and a deer park. The information centre is housed in the attractive 18th-century buildings of Home Farm.

In the late 18th century, Robert Adam started work on remodelling the house. The interior decoration has since been painstakingly restored to his original designs to the extent that this is now the Scottish showpiece of Adam's work. The most outstanding features are the magnificent Oval Staircase and the Round Drawing Room.

i NTS, Culzean Castle

*Continue southwards on the **A719** for 5 miles (8km) to Turnberry.*

Turnberry, Strathclyde

4 This famous golfing centre is dominated by the **Turnberry Hotel**. The golf course sometimes plays host to the British Open.

The remains of the **castle**, which stands by the lighthouse, may have been the birthplace of Robert Bruce. In 1307 Bruce was lured across the Clyde from Arran by a mystic fire and defeated the English force that was occupying the castle, destroying the buildings in the process.

*Leave by the **A77** and follow it northeast for 3 miles (5km) to Kirkoswald.*

BACK TO NATURE

3 *Culzean, Strathclyde* The coastline at Culzean has many different things to look for and is certainly worth exploring. You may find agates on the pebble beach and the rock pools have a wide variety of life in them including sea anemones, sea urchins and butterfish. During the summer there are many seabirds, while during the winter great northern divers might be seen offshore.

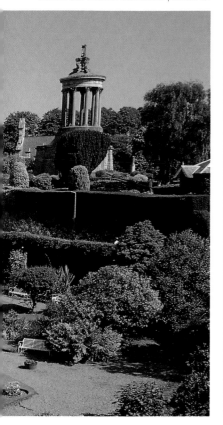

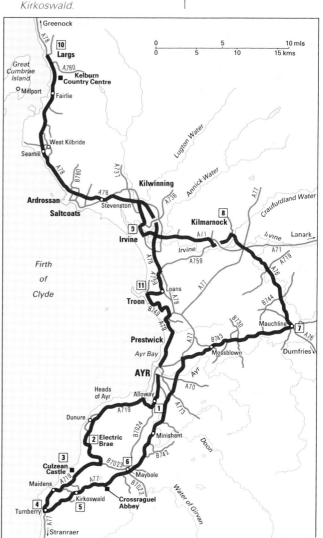

Kirkoswald, Strathclyde

5 Kirkoswald has a number of connections with Robert Burns as his mother's family came from the village. Burns' characters in the poem *Tam o' Shanter* came from Kirkoswald and **Souter Johnnie's Cottage** is on the main road. This thatched house of 1786 was the home of John Davidson, the local 'souter' (shoe-maker), and is now a museum furnished in the style of Burns' day. Burns would have attended the old **Kirkoswald Church**, now a pictures-que ruin within a graveyard in which lie the poet's grandparents and great-grandparents.

*Continue on the **A77** for 4 miles (6km) to Maybole.*

Maybole, Strathclyde

6 Many substantial buildings line the narrow main street, the most strik-ing of which is **Maybole Castle**, a 17th-century Kennedy castle. The castle is featured in an old ballad '*The Raggle Taggle Gipsies*' in which the King of the Gypsies, Johnnie Faa, persuaded a Countess of Cassillis to elope with him. Unfortunately he was caught and hanged while the countess was imprisoned for life in the castle, in the room with the little oriel window that faces up High Street.

Maybole has a long history and its oldest building is the roofless Collegiate Church. Although most of the remaining parts were built in the 15th century, the style is of the 13th and 14th centuries.

Crossraguel Abbey is met a little before Maybole. This relatively small Cluniac monastery (it only had 10 monks in the 15th century) was built in the mid-13th century. It was very badly damaged in the Wars of Independence (1296–1357) and had to be rebuilt. Although roofless, what

Culzean Castle commands a fine position above Culzean Bay. The castle has long been a Kennedy stronghold since they succeeded the Earls of Carrick

walls remain indicate the scale of the establishment. The tall tower house is a particularly unusual building for an abbey.

The towerhouse of **Baltersan Tower** lies between the abbey and the village.

*Continue on the **A77**, then turn right at the **B743** to Mauchline, 18 miles (29km).*

Mauchline, Strathclyde

7 This little town has a number of associations with Robert Burns as he lived at the farm of **Mossgiel**, just north of Mauchline. The most out-standing building is the **National Burns Memorial**; it and the neigh-bouring cottages were built in 1898.

The **church** stands near the centre of the town and in its graveyard lie many people associated with Burns, including several of his children. Burns featured some of them in his poems, like the clockmaker John Brown ('Clockie Brown' in *The Court of Equity*) and a rogue cattle dealer called McGavin who was referred to as 'Master Tootie, alias Laird McGaun' in *To Gavin Hamilton, Esq.* By the churchyard stands the **Burns House Museum** where Burns and his wife set up house in 1788; this also has a collection of local material. Opposite the church stands **Poosie Nansie's Inn**, the setting for *The Jolly Beggars*.

i The Burns Memorial Tower, Kilmarnock Road

*Leave by the **A76** and follow it to Kilmarnock, entering the town by the **A735**.*

Kilmarnock, Strathclyde

8 This industrial town, which is bigger than Ayr, built its affluence on the making of such diverse goods as whisky, carpets and various engin-eering products. Although much of the heart of the town has been changed by the building of modern shops, there are still some very fine buildings, many of them highly ornamented red or white sandstone

structures, erected to reflect the wealth and aspirations of their builders.

The **Dean Castle Country Park** is on the northeast outskirts of the town. The attractive **castle** (based on a 14th-century keep) was a seat of the Boyds, lords of Kilmarnock, and was carefully restored in the 20th century. It houses a collection of arms, armour, tapestries and early musical instruments. The large grounds offer many opportunities for walks.

Kay Park, which is on the eastern side of the Craufurdland Water, has as its centrepiece the tall red sandstone **Burns Monument** which was erected in 1879. A statue of the poet and a small **museum** dedicated to him can also be found here. In 1786 Burns' first work was published and his *Poems chiefly in the Scottish Dialect*, usually known as the Kilmarnock Edition, brought him great fame – and the sum of £20.

ⓘ 62 Bank Street

*Leave by the **A759**. On reaching the **A71** turn west to Irvine, 8 miles (13km).*

Irvine, Strathclyde

9 Irvine has many attractions to its credit but the modern shopping centre, which crosses the River Irvine, dwarfs the older parts of the town and spoils Irvine's riverside location. The town prospered as a busy industrial centre and was once Glasgow's main port before Port Glasgow was developed.

The industrial and maritime history of the town is a good background to the **Scottish Maritime Museum** which has a number of exhibits here. There are boats tied alongside the old harbour wall and these include a 'puffer' (a small cargo boat that served the west coast and its islands), the world's oldest sea-coaster and a

A flotilla of notable sea-going vessels find sanctuary and benevolence at the Scottish Maritime Museum in Irvine. The museum has displays reflecting all aspects of Scottish maritime history and industry

number of other craft, including lifeboats. The museum has exhibitions and displays of various shipbuilding crafts. The prize exhibit is the Victorian engine-shop from Stephen's Linthouse yard in Glasgow which has been re-erected here. This superb tall brick building is supported by the original cast-iron structure that was quite revolutionary when it was constructed in 1872. But industrial museums are not just about factories and their products, they are about the people who made this possible and the museum has restored a shipyard worker's 'room and kitchen' tenement house to what it would have looked like in 1910.

Harbour Street can be followed down the river mouth where the **Pilot House** can be found. This was erected in 1906 with an automatic tide-signalling device which hoisted balls on top of the building to indicate the depth of the water.

The old part of the town on the other side of the river has many interesting buildings to see. Robert Burns came here in 1781 to learn the trade of flax dressing and stayed at No 4 Glasgow Vennel, once the main road to Glasgow. He worked in a 'heckling shop' at No 10. Other places worth looking at include the conservation area of **Hill Street**, the **Townhouse** and the **Burns Club and Museum**.

*Leave by the **A737**, then join the **A78** (towards Greenock). Follow this to Largs.*

FOR CHILDREN

9 *Irvine, Strathclyde* Irvine's **Magnum Centre** is one of Scotland's most popular visitor attractions. It has a swimming pool, ice rink and facilities for sports such as squash, badminton, table tennis and golf practice.

The Clyde Coast is well known for its beaches, including Turnberry, Ayr, Prestwick, Troon, Irvine, Saltcoats, and Ardrossan.

The round tower of Bowen Craig to the south of Largs, aptly nicknamed The Pencil, commemorates the defeat of a Viking fleet here in 1263. As a result the king of Norway lost the Hebrides and the Isle of Man

mass of fine detail carved in locally quarried sandstone. Above it is a painted ceiling which has survived remarkably well down the centuries. The burial ground also contains the burial vault of the local Brisbane family, one of whose members, Sir Thomas Brisbane, was governor of New South Wales in Australia and who gave his name to the state's capital.

At the southern end of the town, a walk along the coast leads to **The Pencil**, a tall monument that celebrates the Battle of Largs of 1263. A Viking fleet under King Haakon of Norway was driven ashore here and roundly defeated by the Scots led by Alexander III.

A regular car ferry crosses over to **Great Cumbrae Island**. The island's 'capital', Millport, has a pretty location looking over to Little Cumbrae Island and the beach is popular with families. Walking right round the island or across its top is a favourite outing and from the roadside **Glaid Stone**, at the summit of the island, there is a wonderful panorama over the Firth of Clyde.

i Promenade

*Return south along the **A78** past Irvine, turning off right on the **A759** to Loans and Troon, 26 miles (42km).*

Troon, Strathclyde

11 This is a pleasant seaside resort, with good beaches and golf courses, one of which is used for the Open. The wide esplanade offers splendid views across the firth towards Arran.

Troon developed as a port in the early 19th century in order to ship out coal from the Kilmarnock coalfield. The quayside wagons were initially hauled by horses but in 1816 a Stevenson steam locomotive was used, an early example of how the railways could be used to transform the country's transport system.

The inner harbour has now been turned into a marina and there is a good viewpoint near it on top of the 'Ballast Bank'. This tall artificial mound was built up over a long time partly by ballast unloaded from coal boats returning from Ireland.

i Municipal Buildings, Troon; Boydfield Gardens, Prestwick

*Leave by the **B749**. Turn right when the **A79** is met and follow this back to Ayr, 8 miles (13km).*

RECOMMENDED WALKS

The parks in Ayr, Culzean and Kilmarnock all offer level walking suitable for pushchairs and wheelchairs. There is also a large network of paths in Eglinton Park at Irvine and opportunities to see swans, roe deer and mink.

Largs, Strathclyde

10 This popular seaside town has a long and attractive promenade giving fine views of the Firth of Clyde. Largs has a reassuringly prosperous air to it and many distinctive sandstone buildings, especially along its front.

One unique structure that is hidden away and tends to be forgotten is the 1636 **Skelmorlie Aisle**, originally part of the parish church. Inside, there is an ornate Renaissance-style monument in the form of an archway which has a

Ayr – Alloway 3 (5)
Alloway – Electric Brae 8 (13)
Electric Brae – Culzean Castle 5 (8)
Culzean Castle – Turnberry 5 (8)
Turnberry – Kirkoswald 3 (5)
Kirkoswald – Maybole 4 (6)
Maybole – Mauchline 18 (29)
Mauchline – Kilmarnock 9 (14)
Kilmarnock – Irvine 8 (13)
Irvine – Largs 19 (31)
Largs – Troon 26 (42)
Troon – Ayr 8 (13)

An alluring shop front on the harbourside at Portpatrick. The shop's decorative title perhaps echoes a more infamous past history for the town

ⓘ Dashwood Square

*Leave by the **A714** and head southwards for 7 miles (11km) to Wigtown.*

Wigtown, Dumfries and Galloway

1 This neat town has a main street wide enough to accommodate the local bowling green and a little park. This central area originally had a very practical use as it was where cattle were herded at night-time to prevent cattle thieves from taking them. At one end of the street are the imposing council offices (this was the county town of the former Wigtownshire) and at the other end is the site of the old mercat (market) cross. The museum is housed in the council offices.

A tall monument will be seen on entering the town. This commemorates the local Covenanters who were executed for their beliefs. The best-known local martyrs were Margaret Wilson and Margaret MacLachlan, who were executed by drowning in the River Bladnoch in 1685. The women's graves can be seen beside the parish church.

The neighbouring village, **Bladnoch**, has Scotland's most southerly distillery and it produces the Bladnoch Single Malt Whisky. Tours round the distillery are available.

*Continue on the **A714**, then turn left on to the **A746** to Whithorn, 11 miles (18km).*

GALLOWAY & THE COVENANTERS

Newton Stewart ● Wigtown ● Whithorn ● Isle of Whithorn
Monreith ● Glenluce ● Port Logan ● Portpatrick
Stranraer ● Girvan ● Loch Trool ● Newton Stewart

Newton Stewart is a pleasant little market town on the banks of the River Cree. Its main street is lined with traditional stone buildings with few modern intrusions to spoil its charm and interest. The street's most impressive building is the tall 18th-century former *town house* which has a square clock tower topped by a cupola roof and a weathercock. The town used to have a prosperous mill industry, but this has declined; however, the *Creebridge Mill*, which specialises in mohair, is open to the public.

The *museum* is housed in a former church in York Street and has many exhibits depicting local history. Outside it is a statue of Robert Paterson, immortalised by the author Sir Walter Scott as the character 'Old Mortality'. Paterson was a stonemason who spent 50 years, from around 1750 to his death in 1800, tidying up the gravestones and memorials of the Covenanters, those Scots who fought against the government for their religious beliefs during the late 17th century.

SPECIAL TO...

Galloway is a good farming area and many farms have fine herds of dairy cows. Much of the milk is processed in local creameries so look out for local cream, cheese and other dairy products. To keep children amused while driving along country roads, get them to look out for 'Belties', the distinctive black and white Belted Galloway cattle.

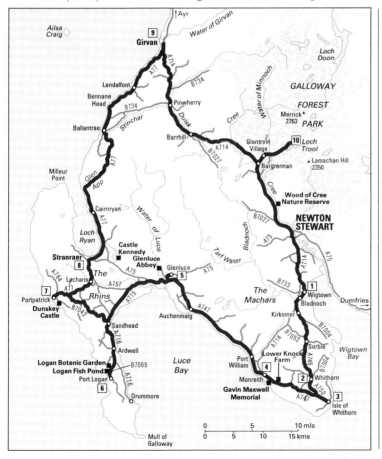

The tattered quayside at Wigtown on the estuary of the River Bladnoch

4 *Monreith, Dumfries and Galloway* **Lower Knock Waterfowl Open Farm** is met before Monreith and as well as waterfowl, it has goats, Shetland ponies, pot-bellied pigs and peacocks. It also has a children's play area and a campsite.

Whithorn, Dumfries and Galloway

2 Whithorn has been an important goal for travellers ever since pilgrims started to visit its important religious buildings. The religious settlement dates from the 5th century when St Ninian established a mission, and this is Scotland's first recorded site of a Christian church. Later, an important priory church was built but this was demolished during the Reformation and the prosperity of the village consequently declined.

Today, the old buildings are in ruins but a Romanesque doorway in what was the **priory** indicates the fine style of architecture that must have existed. Archaeologists have dug deep into the ground in front of the priory and have uncovered valuable evidence of the buildings that must have stood here. They have also unearthed hundreds of skeletons as they had to dig down through the ancient cemetery. These skeletons have provided fascinating clues to the life, health and death of the local people. The continuing investigations, known as the Whithorn Dig, have unearthed many interesting artefacts and these are on display at the site's visitor centre.

i The Whithorn Dig

Leave on the A746, then bear left at the A750. Follow this to the Isle of Whithorn.

Isle of Whithorn, Dumfries and Galloway

3 This picturesquely sited village is not in fact an island at all but does have a well-sheltered harbour which is frequented by fishing boats and many pleasure craft.

Just beyond the harbour is a grassy promontory with a **lookout tower**, and on a fine day Ireland, the Isle of Man, England and possibly even the hills of Wales can be seen. On the seaward side of the village stands the remains of **St Ninian's Chapel**, an early 14th-century church.

Return along the A750, then follow the A747 to Monreith, 9 miles (14km).

Monreith, Dumfries and Galloway

4 Just before the village is reached, a road (left) to the **St Meddan Golf Club** leads to a memorial to Gavin

Maxwell (1914–1969). This is in the form of a bronze otter – Maxwell was a writer and naturalist whose book about otters, *Ring of Bright Water*, was made into a film. A prehistoric spiral 'cup and ring' mark is plainly visible just below the memorial.

*Continue on the **A747**, then turn left at the **A75** (then right at the **A747**) to reach Glenluce, 16 miles (26km).*

Glenluce, Dumfries and Galloway

5 The village developed as a staging post on the busy Stranraer to Carlisle road, and is now a pleasant centre for exploring this corner of the southwest. As if to testify to the village's links with different types of transport, the **motor museum** has vintage cars and motorcycles amongst its exhibits.

Glenluce Abbey, to the northwest of the village, is an impressive ruined Cistercian monastery that was founded around 1190. Its best-preserved structure is the chapter house which has part of the original tiled floor still extant. One of the abbey's interesting architectural details that might be overlooked is the survival of the water-supply system which still has the original jointed earthenware pipes and lidded junction boxes.

*Rejoin the **A75** and head towards Stranraer. Bear left at the **A715**, then follow the **A716** towards Drummore. Turn right at the **B7065** to reach Port Logan.*

Port Logan, Dumfries and Galloway

6 Port Logan is a planned village originally laid out in 1818, with a little pier that has an attractive **light-house** at its end. On the other side of Port Logan Bay, a small cluster of buildings marks the location of the **Logan Fish Pond**, one of the most surprising places to be found in this corner of the country. This is a natural rock pool some 30 feet (9m) deep and 53 feet (16m) in diameter which holds mainly cod and pollack. It was established in 1800 as a fresh seawater 'larder' for nearby **Logan House** but is now a tourist attraction that will

fascinate visitors especially as the fish will take food from the keeper's hand.

Logan Botanic Garden is met just before Port Logan Bay is reached. This is an outstation of the Royal Botanic Garden of Edinburgh and it has a marvellous collection of plants, especially in the well-sheltered walled garden. The warm Gulf Stream keeps the local climate exceptionally mild so many exotic plants such as tree ferns and palms flourish here.

*Return along the **B7065** and **A716** to Sandhead, and turn left at the **B7042**. Turn left at the **A77** for Portpatrick*

Portpatrick, Dumfries and Galloway

7 One of the most attractive of Scotland's small seaside resorts, Portpatrick has a well-sheltered harbour ringed by colourful stone-built houses and hotels. Portpatrick is the nearest Scottish harbour to Ireland and it was once an important base for ferries, fishing boats and troop ships, but today it is mainly pleasure boats that tie up in the harbour.

Although the village is far from the Galloway Hills, many walkers arrive here as this is the start of the **Southern Upland Way**, a long-distance walk of over 200 miles (320km) that stretches right across southern Scotland and ends at Cockburnspath near Dunbar. The Way begins at the back of the harbour.

The ruins of **Old Portpatrick Parish Kirk** stand behind the seafront houses and its most notable feature is its four-storey circular tower. This was probably both a belfry and a beacon for the harbour. The 'Little Wheels' exhibition in the village has displays of model railways from many countries, aeroplanes and various toys, including dolls. Steps from the seafront lead southward to the 16th-century **Dunskey Castle**. This was built around 1510 but was a ruin less than two centuries later.

*Return along the **A77** and follow it for 9 miles (14km) to Stranraer.*

The impressive 12th-century ruins of Cistercian Glenluce Abbey

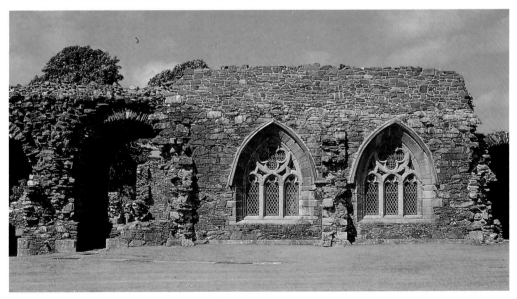

RECOMMENDED WALKS

10 *Loch Trool, Dumfries and Galloway* **Galloway Forest Park** has many marked walks and details about them are available from tourist information offices and the park's Caldons campsite.

The **Southern Upland Way** is met at a number of places in this tour and it provides many opportunities to explore the peace and quiet of the countryside. One good but fairly long section (13 miles/21km) starts at Portpatrick and ends at Castle Kennedy.

BACK TO NATURE

10 *Loch Trool, Dumfries and Galloway* South of Bargrennan, a road goes left to the **Wood of Cree Nature Reserve** which is under the care of the RSPB. The Wood of Cree is one of southern Scotland's best broadleaved woodlands and is sited by the marshy River Cree. Numerous birds may be seen, including the great spotted woodpecker and the tawny owl in the woods; snipe and water rail in the marshes; and the tree pipit and redstart in the scrubland. The reserve has two marked walks, a woodland trail and a scrubland trail.

Stranraer, Dumfries and Galloway

8 Stranraer is the centre for shopping and services in this part of the country, and is also part of an important transport centre. It has a rail link direct to Glasgow, and a busy ferry service to Larne in Ireland.

Near the ferry terminal stands the **North West Castle Hotel**, the former home of Sir John Ross who gained fame exploring the Arctic in search of the Northwest Passage, the sea-route across Arctic Canada. Displays on his exploits are contained in the **museum** which also has exhibitions on the history and agriculture of the area.

Stranraer's main antiquity is the **Castle of St John** which is right in the centre of town. This dates back to 1510 and was later used by the council as a jail. Its rooftop exercise yard gives a fine view of the local scenery.

i Port Rodie Car Park

*Continue on the **A77** for 30 miles (48km) to Girvan.*

Girvan, Strathclyde

9 Girvan is a little seaside town whose beach is popular with families during the summer. It has a busy harbour which is home to a number of fishing boats and some fishermen hire out their craft for fishing trips.

This is probably the best place from which to view the rugged island of

The Bruce memorial at the eastern end of Loch Trool in the Galloway Forest Park. It commemorates a victory over the English by Robert the Bruce in 1307

Ailsa Craig. The island is made from a fine-grained granite which was quarried for the making of high-quality curling stones. The island has a massive colony of gannets with over 10,000 pairs breeding there during the summer.

i Bridge Street

*Leave by the **A714** and at Bargrennan turn left on to the unclassified road to Loch Trool, 27 miles (43km).*

Loch Trool, Dumfries and Galloway

10 The loch sits within the **Galloway Forest Park**, a popular recreational area that attracts walkers, campers and sightseers during the summer. The car park is near **Bruce's Stone**, a memorial to Robert the Bruce, the Scottish king who learned a lesson in persistence from a spider. This overlooks the place where, in 1307, a small group of Scots defeated a force of English soldiers by starting a landslide which buried them.

*Return along the unclassified road to Bargrennan, then turn left on to the **A714**. Follow this road to return to Newton Stewart, 14 miles (23km).*

Newton Stewart – Wigtown **7 (11)**
Wigtown – Whithorn **11 (18)**
Whithorn – Isle of Whithorn **4 (6)**
Isle of Whithorn – Monreith **9 (14)**
Monreith – Glenluce **16 (26)**
Glenluce – Port Logan **16 (26)**
Port Logan – Portpatrick **16 (26)**
Portpatrick – Stranraer **9 (14)**
Stranraer – Girvan **30 (48)**
Girvan – Loch Trool **27 (43)**
Loch Trool – Newton Stewart **14 (23)**

The Galloway Window by Brian Thomas OBE, at the Galloway Deer Museum, Clatteringshaws

ⓘ Whitesands

*Leave by the **A710** (the Solway Coast Road) and follow it for 7 miles (11km) to New Abbey.*

New Abbey, Dumfries and Galloway

1 The village is best-known for the ruins of **Sweetheart Abbey**, or New Abbey, founded in the 13th century as a Cistercian establishment. It is regarded as one of Scotland's most beautiful monastic ruins and, although roofless, it still has massive walls and a fine rose window. The abbey was founded by Dervorguilla, wife of John Balliol, whose son became king of Scotland in 1292. After her husband died, Dervorguilla carried his embalmed heart around with her until she died some 22 years later! She and the heart were buried in front of the high altar – hence the name of the abbey. Dervorguilla also founded Balliol College in Oxford and named it after her husband.

The 19th-century **corn mill** in the village has been restored to working order and is open to the public. It is one of the finest mills of its type in Scotland.

Just outside the village is **Shambellie House**, where the National Museum of Scotland has a museum of costume.

*Continue on the **A710** for 19 miles (31km) to Dalbeattie.*

An exhibition on the acclaimed Scottish poet is displayed at the Burns Centre on the banks of the River Nith, Dumfries

QUEEN OF THE SOUTH

Dumfries ● New Abbey ● Dalbeattie ● Castle Douglas
Kirkcudbright ● Gatehouse of Fleet ● Cairn Holy
Creetown ● Clatteringshaws Loch ● New Galloway
St John's Town of Dalry ● Moniaive ● Dumfries

Dumfries' attractive setting on the banks of the River Nith has earned it the title 'Queen of the South'. This is the region's main town and its fine public buildings reflect the history and prosperity of the local agricultural area. The broad High Street, so typical of a busy market town, is dominated by the *Mid Steeple*, built in 1707.

The town has many connections with Robert Burns. He spent his last days here in what is now *Burns House*; this is preserved as a small museum. The *Burns Mausoleum* is behind *St Michael's Church* and the poet was reinterred there in 1817 along with his wife Jean Armour and several of his children. The *Robert Burns Centre* contains many mementoes of his life.

The *Dumfries Museum* and the *Camera Obscura* stand behind the Burns Centre. The museum has a fine collection of local material and the camera obscura offers a unique view of the town.

SPECIAL TO . . .

The relaxed style of living in the area has attracted many craftsmen and women, and the local craft 'industry' is thriving. The amazing variety of crafts includes fairly common ones such as engraving, pottery and jewellery making as well as more unusual ones like the production of embroidered landscapes, willow furniture and even clogs. Tourist information centres can give details of workshops that are open to visitors.

Dalbeattie, Dumfries and Galloway

2 Dalbeattie was established to exploit the local granite which was quarried at the nearby Craignair quarry. Many of the town's buildings are made from this bright grey stone which sparkles in the sunlight. While some of the stone was used locally, great quantities of it were exported to construct such buildings as London's Bank of England, Liverpool's Mersey Docks, the Eddystone Lighthouse off Plymouth and the Grand Harbour at Valetta, on Malta.

ⓘ Town Hall

*Leave by the **A711**, then turn right at the **A745** to reach Castle Douglas, 6 miles (10km).*

Castle Douglas, Dumfries and Galloway

3 The town was originally called Carlingwark after the local loch, but was renamed in 1792 by a Sir William Douglas after he had acquired the land. Castle Douglas was then developed into an important market town and its horse and cattle fairs helped attract the wealth that built the spaciously laid-out town centre.

The NTS's extensive **Threave Garden** is on the outskirts and it is particularly well known for its spring displays of nearly 200 varieties of daffodils.

Threave Castle stands on an islet in the River Dee. Its four-storey tower was built in the 14th century and it is surrounded by an outer wall of about a century later. One rather unusual feature is that it has the most complete medieval riverside harbour ever discovered in Scotland.

Safe anchorage for the vessels of the Kirkcudbright fishing fleet on the River Dee as it enters the bay at Kirkcudbright

ⓘ Markethill, Castle Douglas; Threave Gardens

*Leave by the **B736** and turn left when the **A75** is met. Turn left at the **A711** and follow this to Kirkcudbright.*

Kirkcudbright, Dumfries and Galloway

4 Kirkcudbright's broad and spacious streets are a delight to stroll along as many old public buildings, such as the 17th-century **Tolbooth**, still stand. The mercat (market) cross of 1610 is on the Tolbooth steps. **McLellan's Castle**, built in the late 16th century, stands near the harbour and dominates this part of the town.

The town has had a long and colourful history, including many connections with sea trading and piracy. In the late 16th century the pirate Leonard Robertson captured an English merchant vessel and sold its cargo to local lairds. When Queen Elizabeth of England complained to King James VI he promised to investigate the matter, which he did by appointing a commission manned by the very lairds who had bought the stolen goods. Such was justice!

The **Stewartry Museum** has a good collection of local material and a section on John Paul Jones. He joined the Union navy and fought against the British during the American War of Independence; his daring exploits included attacks on the British coast. During a 'quiet' time he had the audacity to visit this area in secret.

Broughton House, in High Street, was the home of E A Hornel and is now a museum dedicated to the artist, who died in 1933.

The **Tongland Hydroelectric Power Station** stands on the River Dee, to the north of Kirkcudbright. This is just one of the power stations in the Galloway

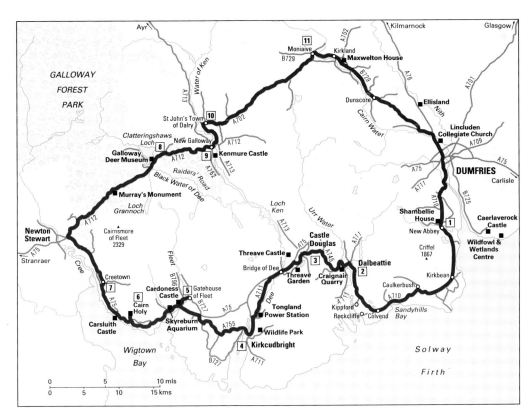

Hydroelectric Scheme and there are organised tours around the buildings. Downstream of the station is the attractive **Tongland Bridge** built by Thomas Telford in 1805.

ⓘ Harbour Square

Leave by the A755 and turn left at the A75. Turn right at the B796 to reach Gatehouse of Fleet.

Gatehouse of Fleet, Dumfries and Galloway

5 This was once a prosperous spinning and weaving village but it is now quiet and rather peaceful. There are numerous hotels, one of which, **The Murray Arms**, was where Robert Burns wrote *Scots Wha Ha'e*.

Cardoness Castle is just outside the village. This was built in the 15th century by the McCullochs and stands in a prominent position overlooking the Water of Fleet.

ⓘ Car Park

Return along the B796 and turn right at the A75. Follow this towards Creetown. Turn right at a narrow signposted road to Cairn Holy, 8 miles (13km).

Cairn Holy, Dumfries and Galloway

6 There are two monuments at Cairn Holy. These were used well over 3,000 years ago as burial sites and for ceremonies of some kind. **Cairn Holy I** is particularly impressive, with its pillared façade and two tombs. The tombs would have originally been covered by a massive cairn of boulders but these were later removed, probably by farmers seeking easily obtained building stones.

Return to the A75 and turn right. Leave the A75 on the right at the signposted road to Creetown.

Creetown, Dumfries and Galloway

7 Creetown is another 'granite town', with many of its buildings made of the local grey stone. The **Gem-Rock Museum** is sited in a former school and has a marvellous collection of minerals, fossils and many other exhibits from all over the world.

Carsluith Castle will be seen on the left before entering Creetown. This started off as a rectangular tower in the 15th century but later additions gave it an L-shape and a balcony. It fell into ruins after 1748.

Rejoin the A75 and turn right. Turn right at the A712 to the Deer Museum at Clatteringshaws Loch (Galloway Forest Park).

Clatteringshaws Loch, Dumfries and Galloway

8 This artificial loch is surrounded by moorlands and conifers and is within the boundary of the **Galloway Forest Park**. The park is home to many interesting animals and there are herds of wild goat and deer on the southern shore of the loch. The **Galloway Deer Museum** has lots of information on the wildlife, geology and history of the area and close by it is a reconstructed Romano–British hut from around AD200–300.

The road to the loch passes below the tall obelisk called **Murray's Monument**. This stands as a testament to the talent of Alexander Murray (1773–1813), the son of a local shepherd who became Professor of Oriental Languages at Edinburgh University. The house where he was born is signposted from the road.

Near the museum, the **Raiders' Road** goes off to the right through the forest and follows an old cattle rustlers' route. Deer may be seen here and if you are very lucky you may

BACK TO NATURE

Dumfries, Dumfries and Galloway The **Wildfowl and Wetlands Centre** at Caerlaverock, southeast of Dumfries, is closed to visitors during the summer until 1992 as the land is managed to provide ideal feeding for thousands of birds that come here during the remainder of the year. Over 12,000 barnacle geese, plus many other birds such as pink-footed and greylag geese, whooper and Bewick's swans and various species of ducks are regular visitors. The centre's hides and observation tower are located at **Eastpark farm**, which is reached from the **B725**.

The Old Bridge over the Nith at Dumfries. Of five bridges, this is the oldest, built by Lady Dervorguilla, foundress of Sweetheart Abbey

see an otter; buzzards, sparrowhawks and ravens can also be spotted.

*Continue on the **A712** for 6 miles (10km) to New Galloway.*

New Galloway, Dumfries and Galloway

9 This quiet little village stands above the Water of Ken. South of it stands 16th-century **Kenmure Castle** which used to be an imposing house until partly dismantled in the 1950s.

*Leave by the **A712**, then turn left at the **A713** to reach St John's Town of Dalry, 3 miles (5km).*

St John's Town of Dalry, Dumfries and Galloway

10 The attractive main street in this pleasant village is lined with whitewashed cottages, at the top of which can be seen a peculiar little stone seat known as **St John the Baptist's Chair**. There is no evidence that the man himself ever sat upon it, but one of Sir Walter Scott's friends found the legend intriguing enough to try and remove it. The **Southern Upland Way** follows the main street and passes the chair on its long coast-to-coast journey between Portpatrick and Cockburnspath.

The **church**, erected in 1831, has several interesting gravestones, some bearing a skull and crossbones or an hourglass. The most notable one is the horizontal **Covenanters' stone** (to

the Auchencloy Martyrs) in the corner of the churchyard, inscribed with the story of their shooting by Claverhouse.

*Leave by the **A702** and follow it for 11 miles (18km) to Moniaive.*

Moniaive, Dumfries and Galloway

11 Moniaive was the birthplace of James Renwick, who was hanged in Edinburgh and was the last of the Covenanter martyrs. A monument to him has been erected at the edge of the village.

To the east, beyond Kirkland, stands **Maxwelton House**, the birthplace and home of Annie Laurie, about whom a famous ballad was composed. The original song was written around 1700, although a later version was penned in 1835. The house was built onto a 14th-century castle and houses a small **museum**.

*Continue on the **A702**, then turn right at the **B729**. Turn right at the **A76** and follow this back to Dumfries, 17 miles (29km).*

Bottles and containers from the past at the Gladstone Court Museum in Biggar

SEARCHING FOR GOLD

Lanark ● New Lanark ● Biggar ● Wanlockhead
Sanquhar ● Douglas ● Strathaven ● Hamilton ● Blantyre
Bothwell Castle ● Craignethan Castle ● Lanark

ℹ️ Horsemarket, Ladyacre Road

Follow the local signs from the market for 1 mile (2km) to the village of New Lanark.

New Lanark, Strathclyde

1 The village is set in the magnificent wooded gorge of the River Clyde and within walking distance of Lanark itself.

During the 18th century Richard Arkwright and David Dale visited the site and soon began establishing cotton mills here, with water power provided from Dundaff Linn, one of the smallest of the Falls of Clyde. At the beginning of the 19th century, Dale's son-in-law Robert Owen developed what was then the country's biggest cotton mill with over 2,000 people in the village, into a superb example of how an industrial undertaking could benefit the local people. The buildings were well constructed and spacious (for that time) and he took on pauper apprentices and housed and educated them. He also built the quaintly named Institute for the Formation of Character. Many of his ideas, including his refusal to use child labour, were revolutionary; what was even more astounding to other mill owners was that his ideas worked and his mills were well-run, efficient and profitable.

Owen's bold experiments are celebrated in the visitors' facilities that occupy some of the old mill buildings. There are fascinating tales of what life was like in the mills and insights into how the Lowland and Highland Scots adapted to the arrival of the industrial age.

*Return to Lanark, then leave by the **A73**. Turn left at the **A72** and the **A702** and follow this to Biggar, 13 miles (21km).*

Biggar, Strathclyde

2 Biggar's main street is even wider than Lanark's, a fact that may have encouraged the saying 'London's London, but Biggar's Biggar!'

For such a compact place, Biggar has a remarkable number of interesting places to visit. The oldest is **Boghall Castle**, now a ruin but once a substantial fortification that was besieged by both Regent Moray and Oliver Cromwell. The most unusual building in the village houses the **gas works** which are the oldest surviving rural gas works in the country, built in 1839.

The **Gladstone Court Museum** in the main street contains a number of replica shops, a schoolroom, a bank and a telephone exchange, scenes which portray life in Victorian Biggar. Further down the street can be seen the small footbridge called the **Cadgers Brig**. Legend has it that William Wallace crossed this in 1297 disguised as a cadger (a pedlar) to spy on the English army that was camped nearby.

On one of the higher parts of the village stands **St Mary's Church**, founded in 1546 as the last pre-Reformation church in Scotland.

The main feature of Lanark is its broad main street where markets were once held. At the bottom of the street are the old *Tolbooth* (1778) and the 18th-century *Church of St Nicholas*. The church tower houses what is said to be the oldest bell in Europe, first cast in 1110, and above the church door stands a statue of William Wallace.

Wallace is thought to have lived in nearby Castlegate before being caught up in the struggle against the English. The centre of that town is worth exploring as there are many attractive 18th- and 19th-century buildings in the High Street and neighbouring streets, which are connected by old passage-ways called wynds.

Lanark is an important centre for the surrounding prosperous agricultural area and a visit to the market is always entertaining. Visitors who arrive in June will have the opportunity of witnessing the Lanimer celebrations, an old custom which originates from the annual inspection of the burgh boundaries.

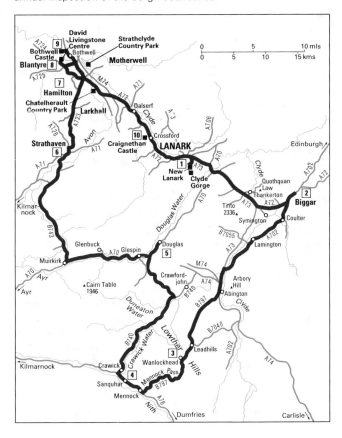

Mine and the **Wanlockhead Beam Engine**. Guided tours into the **Loch Nell Mine** are available and the history of the mines and of the district is told in the **Museum of Scottish Leadmining**.

🛈 Little Chef Service Area, **A74** northbound, Abington

*Continue on the **B797** and turn right at the **A76** to enter Sanquhar, 9 miles (14km).*

Sanquhar, Dumfries and Galloway

4 Although there is a great deal of farmland around Sanquhar, it has the air of an industrial town and lies on the edge of the district's coal mining area. The ruins of **Sanquhar Castle** lie on the outskirts. The castle was built by the Ross family but sold to the Douglases of Drumlanrig in 1639. One of that family, the 1st Duke of Queensberry, built the mansion of **Drumlanrig** but spent only one night at that place and then retired to Sanquhar Castle.

The finest building in the village is the **Tolbooth**, a splendid Georgian building topped by a clock tower, an octagonal cupola and a weathercock. A double-sided staircase leads to a first-floor entrance.

The busy main street boasts the oldest post office in Britain (1763) and a tall granite obelisk erected to commemorate the two Sanquhar Declarations. These were issued by the Covenanters in defiance of Charles II and James VII (II of Great Britain).

🛈 Tolbooth, High Street

*Continue on the **A76** and turn right at the **B740**. Turn left at an unclassified road before Crawfordjohn; this road leads to Glespin, Douglas and Muirkirk. When this road meets the **A70** turn right and follow this to Douglas, 19 miles (31km).*

RECOMMENDED WALKS

1 *New Lanark, Strathclyde* From New Lanark, it is possible to walk up the **Clyde Gorge** to the dam at the waterfall of **Bonnington Linn**. This magnificent gorge, formed about 12,000 years ago after the last Ice Age, has a number of fine waterfalls, notably **Corra Linn**. The water is used to power a hydroelectric power station, but on certain holiday weekends the station is closed down and the falls are at their most impressive,

3 *Wanlockhead, Dumfries and Galloway* Wanlockhead is on the **Southern Upland Way** and the Way's route can be followed from the village to the summit of Lowther Hill. The strange-looking 'golf ball' building on top of the hill houses radar equipment.

Bygone methods of conveyance exhibited at the Hamilton Transport Museum

Opposite this is the **Moat Park Heritage Centre**, which has displays covering 6,000 years of history in Clydesdale. Behind it lies a small valley in which runs the Biggar Burn and this can be followed upstream to **Greenhill**, a farmhouse that was relocated here, stone by stone, from south of Tinto. This is a Covenanting museum, with relics and mementoes of the 17th century.

🛈 155 High Street

*Leave by the **A702**. Join the **A73** then the **A74/M74** and head southwards. Turn off at the **B797** which leads to Wanlockhead, 20 miles (32km).*

Wanlockhead, Dumfries and Galloway

3 Sitting at an altitude of 1,533 feet (467m), this is Scotland's highest village. With neighbouring Leadhills, Wanlockhead was once a major lead mining centre, hence all the piles of debris that have been left here. Lead was probably mined here in Roman times, but the modern history of the mines started about 1675 and the industry managed to keep going, with varying degrees of success, until the 1950s. Gold has also been found in the area; the largest piece found was nearly 7oz (200g) in weight and is now in the British Museum. Gold-panners sometimes come to the district to try their luck and skill in winning a few flakes from the streams.

A number of buildings associated with the mines, complete with mining equipment, have been preserved and these include the **Pates Knowes Smelt**

Douglas, Strathclyde

5 The village is named after the Douglas family, the most famous member of whom was the 'Good' Sir James, so-called by the Scots because it was he who attempted to carry out Robert the Bruce's wish to have his heart taken to the Holy Land. Unfortunately he never got there, as he was killed in Spain. The English, however, knew him as 'Black Douglas' because he was such a ferocious fighter. His most barbaric act took place here in 1307 when he destroyed his own castle, then occupied by English troops. In a gruesome act that became known as the 'Douglas Larder', he made a great pile of all the food in the captured castle, poured on all the wine, killed all his prisoners and threw their bodies into the mix and set fire to it!

The 14th-century **St Bride's Church**, which has an attractive 16th-century octagonal clock tower, has a mausoleum in which lie the remains of the Good Sir James. The **clock tower** is the oldest working town clock in the country and was supposedly a gift from Mary, Queen of Scots in 1565. However, don't set your watch by its chimes as they sound three minutes before the hour, keeping faith with the Douglas motto 'Never behind'.

> Return along the **A70** and continue on it to Muirkirk. Turn right at the **B743** and follow this to Strathaven.

Strathaven, Strathclyde

6 Strathaven is the site of the 15th-century **Avondale Castle**. Beside it stands the **Town Mill** which ground flour until 1966, but now serves as a theatre and arts centre. The town built its prosperity on the weaving industry and the **John Hastie Museum** contains displays on weaving and ceramics together with mementoes of the

Covenanting times and the Radical Rising of 1820, one of whose leaders was a local man, James Wilson.

i Town Mill Arts Centre, Stonehouse Road

> Continue on the **A723** for 7 miles (11km) to Hamilton.

Hamilton, Strathclyde

7 Although Lanark was the county town of the former Lanarkshire, Hamilton became its administrative centre and its fine public buildings reflect its importance. The **District Museum**, which is housed in a 17th-century coaching inn, has a very good transport section.

The parkland lying between the town and the motorway used to be the site of Hamilton Palace, which had to be demolished in 1927 as the extensive coal mine workings had weakened its foundations. However, the splendid 19th-century **Hamilton Mausoleum** still stands here; it has a very fine cupola and ornate carvings. Inside the building, its 15-second echo is the longest of any building in Europe, a fact that put paid to its original purpose as a chapel.

William Adam also designed the Duke of Hamilton's hunting lodge, **Chatelherault**, and this magnificent building, which overlooks the district, is now the centrepiece of the Chatelherault Country Park. The wooded gorge of the River Avon is impressive and beyond it are the remains of **Cadzow Castle** and some very ancient oaks.

> Leave by the **A724** and follow this for 3 miles (5km) to Blantyre.

Decaying stonework marks the site of the castle at Sanquhar, once owned by the Crichtons, and later by the Douglases. The castle has sadly been neglected following their demise

FOR HISTORY BUFFS

Iron Age people built a number of hillforts overlooking the Clyde Valley and these often have ramparts and ditches that were used as defensive structures. The locations were chosen for their lofty positions as there are good views from them. Notable ones include **Arbory Hill** (east of Abington) and **Quothquan Law** (west of Biggar).

SPECIAL TO...

Although Lanarkshire is the industrial heartland of western Scotland, the Clyde Valley is renowned for its orchards. Plums, damsons, strawberries and raspberries are all grown here and the route along the river is particularly pretty during blossom time. When the fruit-picking season arrives, look out for 'pick your own' notices. Tomatoes are grown in the many greenhouses seen along the valley.

David Livingstone (1813–73) was born in a single-room house in Shuttle Row, Blantyre. The whole row now houses the David Livingstone Centre, displaying his life and work in Africa. From 10 to 24 years of age he was a worker in a cotton factory in the town, and it was here that his desire for missionary work was kindled

Blantyre, Strathclyde

8 Blantyre was the home of the explorer David Livingstone and the David Livingstone Centre relates his exploits, which included the 'discovery' of the Victoria Falls and Lake Nyasa. The centre is based in the row of 18th-century tenements where he was born.

*Return along the **A724**, turn left at the **A725** and join the **B7071** to Bothwell. Bothwell Castle is signposted from the town.*

Bothwell Castle, Strathclyde

9 The outstanding castle, which stands on a rocky promontory above the River Clyde, was partially completed before the outbreak of the Wars of Independence (1296–1357) and was twice besieged and deliberately dismantled to deny it to the English. Later rebuilding in the late 14th and 15th centuries turned it into an impressive structure and the

castle's stronghold, the donjon, has massive sandstone walls 15 feet (5m) thick.

*Return along the **B7071**, heading towards Hamilton. Follow the **A74**, then the **A72** to Crossford. In the village, a signposted road on the right leads to Craignethan Castle, 13 miles (21km).*

Craignethan Castle, Strathclyde

10 Craignethan Castle was built in the 16th and 17th centuries when developments in artillery had made many castles' defence systems obsolete. It was built with new defensive strategies in mind and it features a caponier, a low tunnel in the defensive ditch, that allowed the defenders to rake the ditch with small arms' fire.

*Return to Crossford and turn right. Continue on the **A72** for the 6-mile (10km) return to Lanark.*

Spools of wool ready for working into cloth at the Peter Anderson Mills, Galashiels

ⓘ Church Gate

*Leave by the **A701** and turn right at the **B712** to reach Dawyck Garden.*

Dawyck Botanic Garden, Borders

1 This outstation of the Royal Botanic Garden in Edinburgh was developed from the gardens laid out around **Dawyck House** during the last 300 years. Some of the conifers stand 130 feet (40m) high. Daffodils are the main attraction in the spring, while autumn colour is provided by magnificent beeches and maples. Many unusual rhododendrons and narcissi can be found here.

*Return along the **B712** and turn right at the **A701**. This leads to Broughton, 5 miles (8km).*

Broughton, Borders

2 The John Buchan Centre is dedicated to the life and work of the novelist whose best-known works were *The 39 Steps* and *Greenmantle*. Apart from spy stories, he also wrote biographies of various historical figures such as Sir Walter Scott and Oliver Cromwell. He later became Lord Tweedsmuir and was Governor-General of Canada until his death in 1940.

The nearby **Broughton Gallery** is housed in a building constructed in the style of a 17th-century fortified tower house.

*Continue on the **A701** and turn right at the **A72**. Turn left at the **A721** and right at the **A702**. Follow this to West Linton.*

West Linton, Borders

3 West Linton was once busy with cattle drovers bringing their beasts over the Pentland Hills on their way to buyers in England, but today it is a

TAKING THE WATERS

Moffat ● Dawyck Botanic Garden
Broughton ● West Linton ● Peebles ● Innerleithen
Galashiels ● Yarrowford ● St Mary's Loch
Grey Mare's Tail ● Moffat

The pleasant village of Moffat, now a popular tourist centre, gained importance as a spa after the 17th-century discovery of sulphurous springs. Most of the buildings around the exceptionally wide main street were constructed during this period and many of the hotels date from these coaching days. The bronze statue on the fountain in the middle of the village is known as the *Moffat Ram* and it reflects the importance of sheep farming to the local economy.

The most impressive building is the *Moffat House Hotel*, designed by John Adam for the Earl of Hopetoun in 1751. The *Black Bull Inn* dates back to 1568 and was used as a base by the Marquis of Montrose during the 'Killing Times' when he was hunting down the Covenanters. Robert Burns visited the inn in 1789 and scratched the poem *Epigram on Miss Davies* on one of the window panes. The history of the district is told in the *museum*.

The expansive view towards Hart Fell, lying to the west of Moffat. The fell rises impressively to 2,651 feet (808m) above sea level

BACK TO NATURE

Scotland has a number of spas and Moffat has always been one of the most popular. The water is rather sulphurous – one writer compared it to a 'slightly putrescent egg'! Nevertheless, it has attracted many sufferers afflicted with lung infections, dyspepsia and rheumatism. The waters flow from the local greywacke rock and are derived from the decomposition of fish that were trapped in the sediments. The wells are signposted from the village.

FOR CHILDREN

Horse riding is very popular in the district and facilities are available in a number of places, including Peebles and Bowhill. There are swimming pools in Galashiels and Peebles.

SPECIAL TO...

Many of the towns have a justly famous reputation for producing high-quality knitted goods and many of the mills have their own shops where bargains can be found.
  Although it might be thought that the word 'tweed' (meaning the cloth) comes from the river of the same name that is not so. The word is said to have originated in 1832 from a one-time misreading in London of the word 'tweel' which was the name given locally to one of the types of cloth.

RECOMMENDED WALKS

There is great scope for walking in this area and many parts of the **Southern Upland Way** provide well-marked paths that are straightforward to follow. For those who can organise transport at the end of the walks, the Way offers pleasant outings on the eastern shore of St Mary's Loch, from the loch to Traquair and from Traquair to Galashiels (via the cairns known as the Three Brethren).
  Peebles is the start of the **Tweed Walk**, where a choice of circular walks of different lengths allows walkers to pass **Neidpath Castle** and follow the river upstream, visiting various points of interest; contact the Tourist Information Centre for further details.

Fifteenth-century Neidpath Castle, an early Fraser stronghold on the River Tweed, was battered by Cromwell's artillery during the Civil War

peaceful little place pleasant for strolling.
  The village was famous for its stonemasons, who became the chief gravestone carvers in the area. **Gifford's Stone**, a bas relief on a wall in the main street, shows the stonemason James Gifford and his family. Opposite it is another of his works, the **Lady Gifford Well**, which was carved in 1666.

*Leave by the **B7059**. Turn right at the **A701** and left at the **B7059**. Turn left at the **A72** and follow this to Peebles.*

Peebles, Borders

4 This is certainly one of the Scottish Borders' most impressive towns, with an attractive position beside the River Tweed and a fine array of buildings along both sides of the main street. It developed under the protection of a royal castle and its modern prosperity came from tweed and knitwear.
  The **Chambers Institute** in High Street was given to Peebles by the publisher William Chambers who was born in the town. It dates from the 16th century and houses the war memorial which is in the rear garden. Further along the street stand fine buildings such as the **Old Town House**, the **Country Hotel** and the **Tontine Hotel**. This last-named hotel was financed on the 'tontine' principle, whereby the last survivor of a group of investors fell heir to the property. At the top of High Street, the 15th-century mercat cross stands in the middle of the road.
  One of the town's oldest buildings is the **Old Cross Kirk**, built in the 13th century on the order of King Alexander III after the discovery of a 'magnificent and venerable' cross. From here, Cross Road leads to **St Andrew's Tower**, one of the few remains of a church that was built here in 1195. The surrounding graveyard has some beautifully carved headstones.
  Neidpath Castle stands to the west of Peebles. This substantial five-storeyed building was built in the 14th century and sits on a steep rocky crag overlooking the River Tweed.

ⓘ Chambers Institute, High Street

*Continue on the **A72** for 6 miles (10km) to Innerleithen.*

Innerleithen, Borders

5 The town's wells, which were associated with St Ronan, became very popular in the 19th century, helped enormously by Sir Walter Scott's novel *St Ronan's Well*. The poet James Hogg also played a role in publicising the village as he helped organise the St Ronan's Games from 1827 to 1835. The **wells** can still be visited and are found by following Hall Street and St Ronan's Terrace. This is the oldest spa in Scotland and the present pump-room was built in 1826.

The NTS has taken **Robert Smail's Printing Works** in the High Street under its care. This fascinating little print shop was started in 1840, when the original press was water-powered.

The settlement of **Traquair** is just over a mile (2km) south of Inner-leithen. Its history goes back to Roman times when it was a town of similar importance to Peebles. Today it is best known for nearby **Traquair House** which is one of the country's oldest inhabited houses. Additions were made in the 17th century by the 1st Earl of Traquair after the course of the River Tweed was altered to safe-guard the building's foundations. The most famous features of the house are the intricate wrought iron 'Bear Gates' at the end of a long driveway. These were closed in the 18th century by the

5th Earl, who promised they would not be reopened until another Stuart king was on the British throne.

*Continue on the **A72** for 12 miles (19km) to Galashiels.*

Galashiels, Borders

6 Galashiels gained early importance when it was a hunting seat for the Scottish kings. However, its real growth came when woollen mills used the Gala Water to power their machinery. This is now a busy town and one of the main centres of the Borders' knitwear industry. The story of the town mills is displayed in the **Galashiels Museum and Exhibition** which is housed in the Peter Anderson Mills; tours round these mills are available.

The town's most historic building is **Gala House**, which was started around 1583; it has a fine painted

A loom loaded up with brightly coloured warp threads at the Peter Anderson Mills, Galashiels. Opened in 1983 as a museum, it illustrates the importance of the town's woollen industry; tours available

SCENIC ROUTES

Much of this tour goes through beautiful countryside as it winds its way through the hills of the Southern Uplands. Perhaps the nicest stretches are north of Moffat (look out for the large depression called the Devil's Beef Tub between the Tweedsmuir and the Lowther Hills), and through the valleys of the Yarrow Water and the Moffat Water.

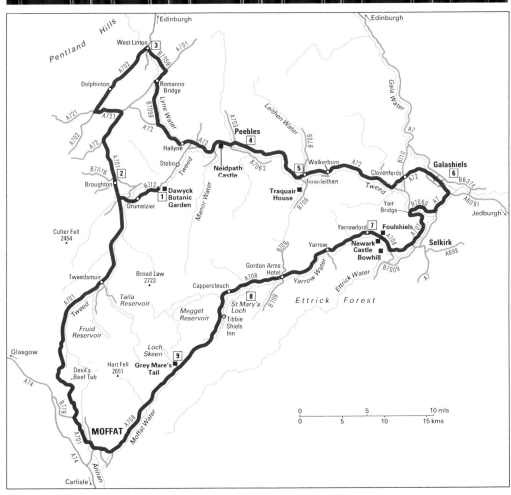

necessarily imply the whole area had trees on it, but that special laws governed its use as a playground for the king and his entourage. However, the forest was inhabited not only by deer and other wild animals; it made a splendid hiding place for thieves, until such time as the king decided to chase them as well! In the 16th century, James V replaced 10,000 deer with an equal number of sheep, greatly increasing the importance of sheep farming and the woollen industry in the area. In conjunction with this step, many trees were felled – thus destroying the oak, birch and hazel forest that had prospered here since the end of the Ice Age.

Foulshiels was the birthplace of the Scots explorer Mungo Park who travelled through West Africa in 1795–6 in search of the source of the River Niger. His exploits were described in his book *Travels in the Interior of Africa* but his second trip into these uncharted lands led to his death.

Bowhill is a very large country mansion built in the early 19th century. It has an outstanding collection of French furniture as well as a large collection of paintings by old Masters including Van Dyck, Canaletto and Gainsborough.

Continue on the A708 for 1,1 miles (18km) to the southern end of St Mary's Loch.

St Mary's Loch, Borders

8 This is one of the largest lochs in southern Scotland and it is a popular place with walkers, boating enthusiasts and anglers. At the southern end of the loch stands a monument to the local poet James Hogg. He was a good friend of Sir Walter Scott and the two of them, along with other literary figures, spent convivial evenings in the nearby **Tibbie Shiels Inn**.

Continue on the A708 for 9 miles (14km) to the car-park at the Grey Mare's Tail waterfall.

Grey Mare's Tail, Dumfries and Galloway

9 Just a short distance from the roadside, the Tail Burn tumbles 200 feet (60m) over the waterfall known as the Grey Mare's Tail. A path runs up the eastern bank of the burn offering different views of the waterfall and the opportunity to explore **Loch Skeen**. Leaflets warn about the dangers of leaving the path. The burn joins the attractive **Moffat Water**, whose valley the road follows towards Moffat. The valley is a magnificent text-book example of a glacial valley, with its U-shape formed as the glacier smoothed the mountainsides.

Continue on the A708 for 10 miles (16km) in order to return to Moffat.

Looking west across St Mary's Loch to the hump of Bower Hope Law

FOR HISTORY BUFFS

Sir Walter Scott, writer of so many 'romantic' stories of Scotland, is connected with many places in this district. He often visited the village of **Clovenfords** and a statue of him stands there; he lived at the house of **Ashiestiel** (further down the Tweed from Innerleithen) from 1804 to 1812; and he had his last meeting with James Hogg at the **Gordon Arms** (east of St Mary's Loch) in 1830.

ceiling of 1635. The mercat cross, which marks the centre of the old town, stands near to Gala House and was erected in 1695. As all the public business of the medieval town was conducted here, this is one of the places involved in the town's **Braw Lads Gathering**, the annual festival during which the boundaries of the town are ridden round on horseback.

The local **war memorial** is in the form of a statue of a mounted Border 'riever'. Although these men have become romanticised figures, they were basically cattle thieves and their activities gave rise to the word 'blackmail' for payment as 'insurance' that livestock would be safe from theft.

i Bank Street

Leave by the A7 (to Selkirk). Turn right at the B7060, then left at the A707 at Yair Bridge. Continue on this road which becomes the A708 near Selkirk. Follow the Ettrick Water and then the Yarrow Water on the A708 to Yarrowford.

Yarrowford, Borders

7 The scattered village of Yarrowford lies by the Yarrow Water, about which poet William Wordsworth wrote no less than three poems! Downstream of the village lie three buildings that are of interest: Newark Castle, Foulshiels and Bowhill.

The name **Newark Castle** signifies that it is the 'new work' which was erected to replace an unsuitable 'auld work'. It was constructed some time before 1423 as a royal hunting lodge in what was known as Ettrick Forest. The term 'forest' in this case does not

The romantic tones of the walled garden echo the general character of Abbotsford House, the home of Sir Walter Scott from 1822 till his death in 1832

ℹ️ Priorwood Gardens

*Leave by the **B6361** and turn left at the **A68**. Cross the River Tweed, then turn first right and first left. Head towards Dryburgh following the **B6356**. Turn right after passing Scott's View and follow this road to Dryburgh Abbey, 6 miles (10km).*

Dryburgh Abbey, Borders

1 Much of the abbey's substantial ruins date from the 12th and 13th centuries and they occupy a wonderfully peaceful position on a horseshoe bend of the River Tweed. Founded in 1150, the abbey suffered at the hands of the English raiders but nevertheless remains the most complete of the Border abbeys. The grave of Sir Walter Scott can be found in the north transept. A short woodland walk leads to a massive 19th-century statue of the Scottish patriot Sir William Wallace.

To the northwest of the abbey (and reached via the B6404) stands the very attractive **Smailholm Tower**. This was erected in the 16th century as a defensive structure, which explains why the few windows it has are very small. There is a marvellous panoramic view from it and ships approaching Berwick once used it as a landmark as it was so conspicuous. During medie-

The intimidating ruins of Melrose Abbey display some of the best and most elaborate traceried stonework in Scotland. The heart of Robert the Bruce is buried somewhere within the church

SCOTT COUNTRY

Melrose ● Dryburgh Abbey ● Jedburgh ● Hawick
Hermitage Castle ● Langholm ● Eskdalemuir ● Ettrick
Selkirk ● Abbotsford ● Melrose

Melrose is an attractive town whose fortunes over the centuries came and went with its abbey. It is now an unspoiled and prosperous resort that stands by the banks of the River Tweed and under the shelter of the Eildon Hills. The centre of the town is built around the market square.

Melrose Abbey, founded in 1136, suffered at the hands of the English on a number of occasions, with Edward II's army sacking it in 1322 and Richard II destroying it in 1385. The majority of the substantial ruins visible today date from the reconstruction of around 1400. Apart from the very impressive church, the *Commendator's House* (now a museum) is worth visiting.

Opposite the abbey is the *motor museum* which has a collection of vintage cars and motorcycles. *Melrose Railway Station*, which was opened in 1849, has not seen a train for many years but this excellent building now has a new lease of life as a craft centre.

SCENIC ROUTES

As the **B6356** makes its way to Dryburgh, there is a wonderful view of the River Tweed and the Eildon Hills at a spot known as **Scott's View**. Sir Walter Scott passed this way on many occasions and always halted here to enjoy the view, describing it as the 'grandest and most extensive panorama in the Borderland'. When he died his funeral cortège made its way past here to Dryburgh Abbey and his horses, without being commanded to, stopped quite naturally at the viewpoint.

SPECIAL TO...

Rugby is not just special to the Borderers – many of them live and breathe the game. Intense rivalry exists between the teams from the various towns and a 'local derby' is always a most enjoyable event to witness. Melrose was where the game of rugby sevens started and its **Sevens' Tournament** in April is the most famous of this type of popular event.

FOR CHILDREN

Pony trekking is popular in the Borders as many good tracks cross the undulating countryside. There are riding facilities at places such as Hawick, Snoot Youth Hostel (west of Hawick), Jedburgh and Selkirk.

As a wet weather alternative, there are swimming pools at Hawick, Jedburgh and Selkirk.

RECOMMENDED WALKS

The Eildon Hills, the three exceptionally attractive hills that rise above Melrose, make up one of the country's best-known landmarks. They are visible from many places and consequently offer good views from their own summits. The usual route up them is from near Melrose Station and starts by following the **B6359**.

val times this area was often attacked by English forces and tall towers were needed to spy on the movements of the enemy and to warn others of the approach of an attacking force. Hence the parapet wall has a watchman's seat and a recess for a lantern, in accordance with an Act of Council in 1587 which stated that castle owners must '*keep watch nyght and day, and burn baillis* (bales) *according to the accoustomat ordour observit as sic tymes upoun the borderis*'. At one time it was owned by Sir Walter Scott's grandfather and Scott used to visit here as a boy; he later featured the tower in *Marmion*.

*Return to the **B6356** and continue following that road. Turn right at the **B6404** and enter St Boswells. Turn left at the **A68** and follow it to Jedburgh, 13 miles (21km).*

Jedburgh, Borders

2 The town's location close to the border meant that it was forever being attacked by the English, and its **castle** was often under siege by the ancient enemy. The locals obviously got rather fed up with all this harassment and managed to persuade the Scottish parliament to pull the castle down in 1409, thus relieving them of the task of having to fight the invaders to defend it! The present building occupying the site is still called the 'castle' but it was built in the 19th century as a jail and is now used as a **museum**.

The other major building in the town is **Jedburgh Abbey**, founded as a priory in 1138. After various attacks by the English, the building was des-

troyed by them between 1545 and 1546. However, the abbey walls still soar skywards and the tower stands as it did when rebuilt in 1504 to 1508.

Mary, Queen of Scots visited the town in 1566 and stayed in the **Spread Eagle Hotel** in High Street which is claimed to be the oldest continually occupied hotel in the country. A fire in the night here forced Mary to leave and she stayed at what is now the **Mary, Queen of Scots' House**, a fine 16th-century fortified house.

i Murray's Green

*Leave by the **B6358**, then join the **A698** for 12 miles (19km) to Hawick.*

Hawick, Borders

3 Hawick is the largest and busiest of the Border towns. Its numerous woollen mills have brought it much prosperity since frame knitting was introduced here and commercialised in 1771. When mechanisation came to the industry, production changed from hose to fine underwear, which as the advertisements of the day put it, 'enjoyed the patronage of many of the crowned heads of Europe'!

Many of the mills stand by the River Teviot, their original source of power. The river also flows past **Wilton Lodge Park**, in which stands the **museum and art gallery** which has displays on Border history, the knitwear industry and natural history.

i Common Haugh Car Park

*Leave by the **B6399**. Just after Hermitage, turn right at the unclassified road signposted to Hermitage Castle.*

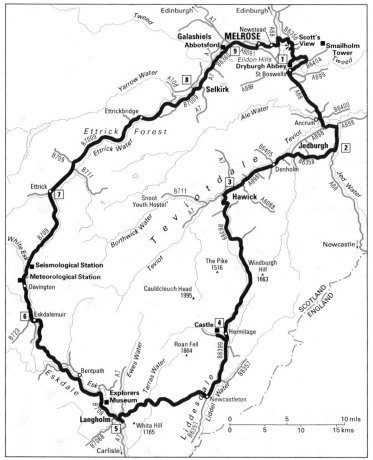

Hermitage Castle, Borders

4 This must be one of the grimmest looking castles in Scotland, with its very small windows and the high arch that joins the east and west towers together. It is also sited on an isolated expanse of moorland, well away from any settlement.

In 1566, when she was holding court at Jedburgh, Mary, Queen of Scots heard that her lover Bothwell was lying wounded in the castle. She rode the 20 miles (32km) there at a furious speed, stayed for a couple of hours then returned, an exertion that cost her a 10-day fever.

*Return to the **B6399** and turn right. Turn right at the **B6357** and enter Newcastleton. Within the village, turn right at the minor road to Langholm and turn left when the **A7** is met in order to enter the town, 17 miles (27km).*

Langholm, Dumfries and Galloway

5 This small town sits at the confluence of the Esk, Ewes and Wauchope waters. There is a fine view of it from the summit of **Whita Hill** (to the east), on top of which there is a monument to Sir John Malcolm. Close to the start of the path to the monument, there is a rather interesting (or bizarre, depending on your taste) monument dedicated to the modern Scots poet Christopher Murray Grieve, who wrote under the pen-name Hugh MacDiarmid.

Another of Langholm's sons was the great engineer Thomas Telford,

---

Jedburgh Abbey, the most complete of the Border abbeys, was founded early in the 12th century and colonised by monks from Beauvais in France. Alexander III was married here in 1285

---

whose most famous designs include the Caledonian Canal, the Menai Straits Bridge and St Katherine's Docks in London. Many roads and bridges in Scotland are also his. Telford started his working life as a stonemason, and an archway, an early example of his own handiwork, can be seen beside the town hall. A memorial to him is sited at **Bentpath**, on the road to Eskdalemuir.

Just north of Langholm, the **Craigcleugh Scottish Explorers Museum** has a large collection of artefacts from many countries visited by Scottish explorers.

ⓘ High Street

*Leave by the **B709** and follow it for 14 miles (23km) to Eskdalemuir.*

Eskdalemuir, Dumfries and Galloway

6 There is a settlement at Eskdalemuir (at the junction of the Langholm and Lockerbie roads), but the name is more commonly used for the great moorland near the upper reaches of the White Esk. To be correct, it used to be a great moorland, but the land is now given over to huge conifer plantations.

The Romans built an important road here, some 24 feet (7m) wide,

---

BACK TO NATURE

Melrose, Borders Melrose's **Priorwood Garden**, which is run by the NTS, specialises in dried flowers. A bewildering variety of plants, both large and small, are grown and dried here and there is always lots of valuable advice to be had on this craft. A small herb garden has also been established and there is an orchard with a wide variety of apple trees, arranged to illustrate the history of the fruit. The monks of Melrose Abbey established their orchard at **Gattonside**, just over the Tweed from the abbey.

A gently meandering stretch of the Ettrick Water near the little village of Ettrick

Many of the Border towns have **Common Ridings**, an annual event when horse riders follow the town's boundaries in an enactment of the ancient tradition of checking the integrity of the boundary. Many of the celebrations have pagan and Christian elements in them; Bacchus is certainly not forgotten in the festivities either. The principal participant in the Common Riding has a variety of different names: in Jedburgh it is the Callant, in Selkirk the Soutar, in Galashiels the Braw Lad and in Kelso the Laddie. Summer visitors should consult the local tourist information centre to find out if there is a riding taking place near them.

and this eventually led to *Trimontium* near Melrose. The most intriguing group of modern incomers were Tibetan abbots who left their country in 1959 and settled here in Johnstone House. The community they founded flourished and they later built one of Scotland's most remarkable buildings, the **Samye Ling Temple**, a colourful four-storey structure. This is the largest Buddhist temple in western Europe and numerous examples of Tibetan art can be seen inside.

The **meteorological station** at Eskdalemuir is sited further along the road. This was originally founded in 1908 to continue the terrestrial magnetism measurements formerly made at Kew (in London). A seismological station has been established nearby.

*Continue on the **B709** for 12 miles (19km) to Ettrick.*

Ettrick, Borders

7 The collection of houses and farms at Ettrick is found where the B709 meets the Ettrick Water at **Ramseycleuch**.

The poet James Hogg was born here and a tall sandstone memorial at his birthplace can be found on the roadside by following the Ettrick Water upstream. Hogg is one of the Borders' most famous characters and was affectionately known as the Ettrick Shepherd. He was first published in 1794 and went on to write many poems, articles and books.

Ettrick's **church** is further upstream and this is where Hogg is buried. Beside his headstone is one inscribed 'Here lyeth William Laidlaw the farfamed Will o'Phaup who for feats of frolic, agility and strength had no equal in his day'. This gentleman was Hogg's grandfather and he was the last man in Ettrick to speak to the fairies.

*Continue on the **B709**, then turn right at the **B7009** to enter Selkirk, 18 miles (29km).*

Selkirk, Borders

8 The town occupies a hilly site where a Tironensian abbey was founded around 1113. The abbey was eventually moved to Roxburgh and then to Kelso so Selkirk never developed as a religious centre like the other Border towns which had their splendid abbeys. As the town grew it became famous for its shoemaking, to the extent that its burgesses were given the name 'souters' (Scots for 'shoemakers'). This trade died out and Selkirk's modern prosperity is based on the woollen mills beside the Ettrick Water.

The centre of the town is at the triangular-shaped marketplace dominated by a statue of Sir Walter Scott. Behind is the old **courtroom** which contains his bench and chair from the time when he was Sheriff of Selkirkshire.

The local **museum** in **Halliwell's House** is to the west of the marketplace and is found by passing through a narrow lane. The museum has an excellent display of local material including the reconstructed interior of an old ironmonger's shop.

To the east of the marketplace, and past the statue of the explorer Mungo Park, is the **Flodden Memorial**, dedicated to the local men who perished at the Battle of Flodden in 1513. The statue is of a man called Fletcher, reputedly the only Selkirk man out of 80 to return from the battle, carrying a captured English standard.

ℹ️ Halliwell's House

*Leave by the **A7** and head towards Galashiels. Turn right at the **B6360** in order to reach Abbotsford.*

Abbotsford, Borders

9 Sir Walter Scott bought the site on which he built Abbotsford in 1811. The house took a long time to complete as he kept adding bits on, eventually ending up with a great variety of styles. Basically, it is of Scots baronial style but he included a 16th-century door from Edinburgh's Tolbooth, a copy of a porch at Linlithgow Palace and even medieval gargoyles. He was a romantic in his architectural taste as well as his writings.

Scott was a lawyer and served as Sheriff in Selkirk. He assiduously collected and wrote down the oral tradition of the old Border tales that had been handed down through the generations, thus ensuring that many of them were preserved. He also began to write his own material and started to make a reputation for himself as a poet and then as a novelist. His best-known works include *Kenilworth*, *Redgauntlet* and *Ivanhoe*. Unfortunately, the financial collapse of a publisher landed him with huge personal debts and he tried to work himself out of debt; sadly this pace of work led to his death in 1832.

*Continue on the **B6360** and turn right at the **A6091** for 3 miles (5km) in order to return to Melrose.*

Melrose – Dryburgh Abbey **6 (10)**
Dryburgh Abbey – Jedburgh **13 (21)**
Jedburgh – Hawick **12 (19)**
Hawick – Hermitage Castle **16 (26)**
Hermitage Castle – Langholm **17 (27)**
Langholm – Eskdalemuir **14 (23)**
Eskdalemuir – Ettrick **12 (19)**
Ettrick – Selkirk **18 (29)**
Selkirk – Abbotsford **5 (8)**
Abbotsford – Melrose **3 (5)**

Abbotsford House, Sir Walter Scott's creation of an 'ancient' property of varying architectural styles from what had previously been a modest farmstead

2 days – 148 miles (239km)

THE BORDER COUNTRY

Edinburgh ● Gullane ● North Berwick ● Tantallon Castle
Preston ● Dunbar ● Cockburnspath ● St Abbs
Eyemouth ● Duns ● Coldstream ● Kelso ● Lauder
Crichton Castle ● Edinburgh

Few cities can match the magnificence of Edinburgh's city centre – *Princes Street*, its gardens and the view up towards the castle. *Edinburgh Castle* stands at the top of the *Royal Mile*, four streets that run down to the magnificent *Palace* of *Holyroodhouse*. Along the Mile can be seen the 'lands', blocks of flats dating from medieval times and *Gladstone's Land*, built after 1617, is under the care of the NTS.

Edinburgh's Georgian architecture with elegant buildings, broad streets, squares and crescents, makes this one of the world's most successful examples of town planning. To the east of Princes Street stands *Calton Hill*, topped by the unfinished *National Monument*, which offers a wide panorama of the city and the Firth of Forth. But by far the best view of Edinburgh is from *Arthur's Seat*, a volcanic hill standing some 823 feet (251m) above sea level.

Many of Scotland's national collections are housed in Edinburgh, including the *National Gallery of Scotland*, the *Royal Scottish Museum* and the *Royal Museum of Scottish Antiquities*.

A fine Norman archway among the remains of 12th-century Kelso Abbey, founded by David I. It was destroyed in 1545 by the Earl of Hertford

ℹ️ 3 Princes Street

*Leave by the **A1** and turn left at the **A198** for 21 miles (34km) to reach Gullane.*

Gullane, Lothian

1 Gullane is renowned as a golfing centre, with a number of courses including a championship course at nearby **Muirfield**. There is a **Heritage of Golf Museum** by the links.

Further east, the centre of the old village of **Dirleton**, claimed to be the most beautiful village in Scotland, is dominated by the grand **Dirleton Castle** which dates back to the 13th century. Perched on top of a rocky platform, it has massive towers and was defended by a moat at least 50 feet (15m) wide.

*Continue on the **A198** for 5 miles (8km) to North Berwick.*

North Berwick, Lothian

2 This seaside golf resort is dominated by the nearby 613-foot (187m) **North Berwick Law**, which offers fine views over the town and the coast.

The town's main antiquity is the ruin of the old church of **St Andrews**, where in 1591 the story goes that a gathering of witches and wizards was addressed by the Devil in the form of a black goat. They sought the death of James VI and a number of these 'plotters' were subsequently brought to trial and burned at the stake. The devil (who may have been the heavily disguised Earl of Bothwell) escaped a similar fate.

ℹ️ Quality Street

*Continue on the **A198** and turn left at a signposted minor road to Tantallon Castle, 3 miles (5km).*

An impressive view of Edinburgh from Calton Hill looking straight down the city's main artery, Princes Street, with the castle standing high up on the left

Although the tour does not meet any of the Borders' mill towns, there are plenty of sheep. This region is the home of Scottish sheep farming and today the main breeds are the Blackface and the Cheviot. The hills are usually rounded and grassy and the Blackface are well able to survive on the inferior high pastures. However, their fleece is relatively coarse and is generally suited to carpet manufacture rather than clothes. Other features of farming life to look out for are the drystane (drystone) dykes that separate the sheep pastures and the drystane stells (enclosures) that shepherds drive their flocks into.

FOR HISTORY BUFFS

Edinburgh, Lothian **Roslin Chapel**, to the south of Edinburgh, is one of the most ornamented churches in the country. It dates from the middle of the 15th century and has all kinds of embellishments carved out of the stone. Its most famous carving is the **Prentice Pillar**, carved by an apprentice when his master was away. So beautiful was it that when the master saw it he killed the lad in a jealous rage – so the story goes.

Only a few miles away stands a completely different kind of attraction, the **Lady Victoria Colliery** at **Newtongrange**. The Lothian area was an important coal mining district and this mine, built between 1890 and 1894, is part of the Scottish Mining Museum.

FOR CHILDREN

There are a number of good beaches, notably at Gullane Bay. Indoor swimming pools are located in Kelso, Duns and Eyemouth and there is an outdoor one at North Berwick. Pony trekking is available at Earlston, Ford (near Pathhead) and Westruther (east of Lauder).

SCENIC ROUTES

After the road turns inland from the coast, it passes along the northern border of the rich agricultural area known as the Merse, where there are pleasant little agricultural villages and traditional stone-built farm buildings. To the north lie the vast open spaces of the moors of the Lammermuir Hills.

Tantallon Castle, Lothian

3 The castle stands in a spectacular clifftop position, with three sides protected by the sea and the fourth by immensely thick walls. Two great sieges took place here: the first ended by negotiation (the attackers had run out of gunpowder!) and in the second, General Monk attacked it for 12 days in 1651, damaging the towers.

This is the best place on the mainland to view the **Bass Rock**. The island has huge numbers of gannets breeding there and the colony is so important that the birds' scientific name *Sula bassana* comes from the island.

> Return to the **A198** and continue southwards. Turn right at the **B1407** to enter Preston.

Preston, Lothian

4 On the outskirts of the village stands the charming water-driven **Preston Mill**, built in the 18th century. Originally a meal mill, the unusual design of its kiln has similarities with an English oast house. The attractive cluster of buildings is constructed of orange sandstone rubble and roofed with traditional east coast pantiles.

A short walk leads to the **Phantassie Doocot**, a dovecot which once housed some 500 pigeons.

> Leave by the **B1047** and turn left on to the **B1377**. Turn left at the **A1**. Turn left at the **A1087** to Dunbar.

Dunbar, Lothian

5 This popular seaside resort is now a rather peaceful place, a far cry from the turbulent times when its **castle** was of some importance. The castle

Preston Mill, the oldest working water-driven meal mill to survive in Scotland. It was last used commercially in 1957

was eventually sacked by Cromwell in 1650 and its walls torn down, the stones being used to improve the harbour. The remains sit quite forlornly by the harbour entrance. The attractive harbour is home to a busy fishing fleet and there is a nearby **lifeboat museum**. Conservationist John Muir was born in Dunbar in the mid-19th century.

[i] Town House, High Street

> Continue on the **A1087** and turn left at the **A1**. Follow this to Cockburnspath, 8 miles (13km).

Cockburnspath, Borders

6 The position of this village so close to the border has meant a turbulent and rather troubled history. This was an important stopping point for horse-drawn coaches (a mode of travel which peaked in the 19th century) and the layout of the village and its marketplace owes much to this time. The **parish church** is worth a look; it has a fine tower in the middle of the west gable and an unusual sundial on the southwest corner.

The mercat cross is the finishing point of the **Southern Upland Way**, the long distance footpath that starts at Portpatrick, over on the west coast. By following the Way from its terminus, the path leads to a group of houses at **Cove**, below which is the picturesque Cove Harbour. The harbour is reached by going through a tunnel cut into the cliff; this was made in the 18th century and was con-

Edgar, the 13th-century priory church was built on a site that had a religious house way back in the 7th century. Life could hardly have been peaceful for those that stayed here during the frequent outbreaks of hostilities, as the monks were subject to the English king and the priors to the Scots king!

Return along the **B6438** *to Coldingham and turn left at the* **A1107**. *Turn left at the* **B6355** *to enter Eyemouth.*

Eyemouth, Borders

8 This interesting and busy fishing port has regular fish markets which are worth visiting. This is home to a large fleet and the local people have been connected with fishing for a very long time. The town's saddest day came on 14 October 1881 when a sudden gale blew up and 129 local fishermen were drowned, some of them in full sight of anxious families watching from the shore. The Eyemouth **museum** tells the story of the tragedy.

i Auld Kirk

Take the **B6355** *south, then follow the* **A6105** *which leads to Duns, 14 miles (23km).*

Duns, Borders

9 This long-established village, with its well-built stone houses, makes a useful stopping point for touring this part of the Borders. This was the home town of the world motor-racing champion Jim Clark, who died in a race in Germany in 1968; a small **museum** has mementoes of his short but fascinating life.

Leave on the **A6112** *for 12 miles (19km) to reach Coldstream.*

Coldstream, Borders

10 Coldstream stands on the banks of the River Tweed, which at this point marks the border with England.

BACK TO NATURE

7 *St Abbs, Borders* The cliffs at St Abb's Head are home to countless kittiwakes, guillemots, razorbills and other seabirds. A marked path starts from just before St Abbs village and leads past the bird cliffs, allowing a very good view of the colonies – but stick to the path!

The small harbour at the fishing village of St Abbs, the only accessible point on a cliff-bound stretch of coastline

---

nected to cellars probably used for curing and barrelling fish, and possibly by smugglers.

Continue on the **A1** *and turn left at the* **A1107**. *At Coldingham, turn left at the* **B6438** *and follow this to St Abbs.*

St Abbs, Borders

7 This neat little fishing village is now a resort, often busy with divers who come to explore the local bays.
Nearby **Coldingham** has an ancient **priory**. Founded in 1098 by King

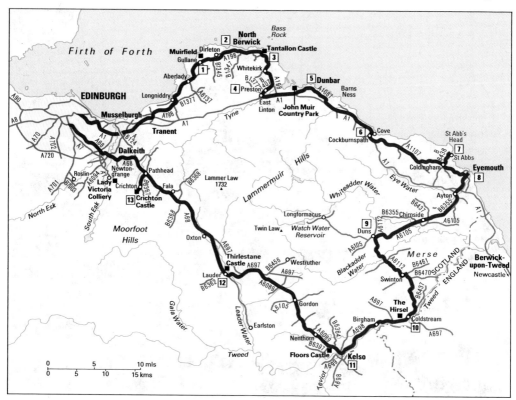

This border was adopted in 1018. The river is crossed by a magnificent seven-arch **bridge** and on the Scottish side a toll house was the east coast equivalent of Gretna Green, a place where marriages could take place with the minimum of delay.

Like so many other little towns in the Borders, Coldstream has a wealth of well-built houses, especially along its main street. The Market Square is a little off this street and in it can be found the **regimental museum** of the Coldstream Guards.

Outside Coldstream stands the **Hirsel Homestead Museum** comprising a museum, craft centre and walks in the estate. Hirsel is the seat of the Earls of Home.

ⓘ Henderson Park

*Leave by the **A697** and turn left at the **A698** to reach Kelso.*

Kelso, Borders

11 Kelso has one of the most attractive town centres in the Borders, with a huge open square that has often been likened to that of a French town. The town stands at the confluence of the rivers Teviot and Tweed and from the fine bridge which crosses the Tweed is a good view of **Floors Castle**, home of the Duke of Roxburghe, a huge mansion built by William Adam between 1721 and 1725.

Kelso Abbey was once the Borders' greatest abbey but only the west end of it stands today. It was founded here in 1128 but its position on the 'invasion route' meant that it suffered frequent attacks.

ⓘ Turret House

*Leave by the **A6089** and turn left at the **A697**. Turn left at the **A697** and right at the **A68**. Follow this to Lauder.*

Lauder, Borders

12 This attractive small town has a wide main street in the middle of which stands the **Tolbooth**. This was originally built in 1318 and the ground floor was used as a jail up to 1840. Lauder's **parish church** is an interesting centrally planned structure in the form of a Greek cross with an octagonal steeple and four arms; it is dated 1673.

Impressive **Thirlestane Castle** stands close to the town. This dates from the end of the 16th century but there have been many alterations since then. The castle houses the **Border Country Life Museum**.

The village of **Earlston** lies only a few miles south of Lauder. This was Ercildoune in medieval days and the home of Thomas the Rhymer who lived during the 13th century. His ability to see into the future was reckoned to be a gift from the Queen of the Fairies with whom it was believed he stayed for a number of years.

*Continue on the **A68** to Pathhead, then turn left at the **B6367** to Crichton Castle.*

Crichton Castle, Lothian

13 Crichton was originally the home of the Earl of Bothwell, the ill-fated third husband of Mary, Queen of Scots. The ruins of this substantial structure stand on the edge of Middleton Moor and above the Tyne Water. It dates from the 14th century and one architectural curiosity is a Renaissance-influenced **wall** erected in the late 16th century. This is an arcade of seven bays topped by diamond-patterned stonework and is almost unique in the country.

Crichton's **church** is a fine building which was restored in 1896.

*Return along the **B6367** to Pathhead. Turn left and follow the **A68** in order to return to Edinburgh.*

Edinburgh – Gullane **21 (34)**
Gullane – North Berwick **5 (8)**
North Berwick – Tantallon Castle **3 (5)**
Tantallon Castle – Preston **6 (10)**
Preston – Dunbar **6 (10)**
Dunbar – Cockburnspath **8 (13)**
Cockburnspath – St Abbs **12 (19)**
St Abbs – Eyemouth **5 (8)**
Eyemouth – Duns **14 (23)**
Duns – Coldstream **12 (19)**
Coldstream – Kelso **9 (14)**
Kelso – Lauder **18 (29)**
Lauder – Crichton Castle **16 (26)**
Crichton Castle – Edinburgh **13 (21)**

The surviving ruin of the once mighty tower of Kelso Abbey, showing fine Norman detail

RECOMMENDED WALKS

7 *St Abbs, Borders* St Abb's Head offers a pleasant and interesting walk. Other good walks can be found in the **John Muir Country Park** (west of Dunbar) and at **Barns Ness** (on the coast, southeast of Dunbar).

9 *Duns, Borders* Inland, a road can be followed from Duns to the settlement of **Longformacus** and then up to the **Watch Water Reservoir**. From there, the route of the Southern Upland Way can be followed to the two massive **Twinlaw Cairns**. The view is impressive, and the island of Lindisfarne can be seen from the top.

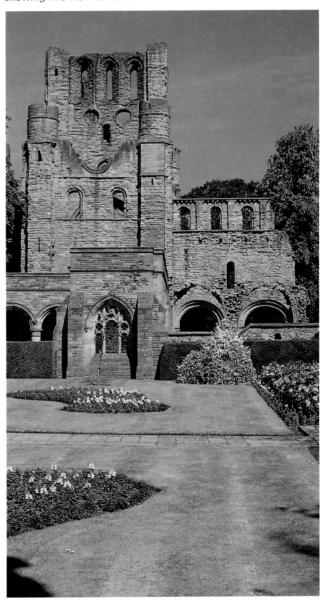

CENTRAL SCOTLAND

The great firths of the Clyde, the Forth and the Tay have narrowed the middle of Scotland to a thin neck of land only 30 miles (48km) wide. This is where the majority of the Scots live, in an area rich with a history that spans many millennia. Bronze Age cemeteries, medieval castles, historic battlefields and bizarre architectural follies all have their statements to make about their builders' views of the world and how they lived – and died.

Much of the region's history has been bloody. Land- and sea-borne invaders attacked, plundered and wrought destruction. Many invaders stayed and left their mark, often introducing foreign influences – some good, some bad – that have added to the common heritage of the modern Scottish nation. The Celts, Vikings, French and the peoples of the countries washed by the Baltic and the North Sea have all contributed to the country's history, but it has been the English who, despite being 'the auld enemy', have in so many ways changed the country – and also radically influenced how the Scots see themselves today as a nation.

Central Scotland's modern prosperity was based on the Industrial Revolution and many would argue that this was where that important period of history began. One of the world's first major ironworks, the first major use of efficient steam engines, the world's biggest shipbuilding industry – all of these were based right here.

Although the manufacturing industry has declined, the outstanding engineering marvels of Scotland are now today's tourist attractions in their own right. Eighteenth-century ironworks, 19th-century canals and the world's most famous railway bridge – spanning the Firth of Forth – are all showpieces of an industrial nation's genius for design. The region can also boast many architectural gems: the rich legacy of Victorian buildings in Glasgow, the grand country houses designed in Scots baronial style and the distinctive cottages of farmer and fisherman all display a very Scottish flavour. Glasgow itself has enjoyed regeneration in recent years, and now takes its rightful place as one of Europe's most lively and interesting cities.

But it is the quality of life that matters more than bricks and mortar and visitors will soon discover that one of the greatest attractions of the populated areas is their closeness to the magnificent hills and glens of the Highlands. The hills are never far away and even Glasgow, the country's industrial 'capital', has the Campsie Fells only a few miles from its centre. In summer it is not unknown for enthusiastic rock climbers from Glasgow to head for the hills after work, climb a few 'pitches' in the peace and quiet of the Trossachs and then head home as the sun is setting!

Tour 8

Although this route is only a couple of hours' drive away from the industrial heartland of Scotland, it nevertheless encompasses some superb highland scenery. The highly indented coast-line, backed by 3,000-foot (900m) high hills, provides a backdrop to some fascinating places like the 5,000-year-old cairns at Kilmartin, medieval castles and the picturesque setting of the Crinan Canal.

Tour 9

The Cowal peninsula is made up of a group of narrow peninsulas shaped like a grasping hand trying to grip the northern shore of the island of Bute. The narrow, twisting roads of Cowal give ever-changing vistas over the sea lochs and the great estuary of the Firth of Clyde, the busy waterway that linked the local communities before the arrival of the internal combustion engine.

Tour 10

The 'border' between the Highlands and the Lowlands is studded with lochs gouged out of the landscape by long-lost glaciers. Some of the country's best-known lochs are found here, like Loch Lomond and Loch Tay, and today's visitors follow in the footsteps of the 19th-century tourists, eager to see the 'wild' scenery so romanticised by Sir Walter Scott.

Tour 11

This historic corner of Scotland has an abundance of important buildings that armies fought over for centuries. Abbeys, grand palaces and austere castles all existed as royalty's prizes and Stirling, the 'gateway to the Highlands', was the jewel in the crown that invaders dearly sought and the Scots defended to the last. The battlefields found here testify to the lives sacrificed in the centuries of turmoil. But some places can often evade change and the small coastal town of Culross has left a rich legacy in its preserved buildings that time just passed by.

Tour 12

A rich agricultural area, Strathmore provides the background to this tour which skirts the southern limits of the Grampian Highlands. Prosperous farming communities, busy east coast fishing ports and the bustling industrial town of Dundee all add their interest. In many ways this area is one of Scotland's 'hidden gems', as it is often missed by many visitors more intent on heading straight for the Highlands.

*Right: a statue of Robinson Crusoe
in Lower Largo commemorates
Alexander Selkirk, Defoe's original
model for the book, who was born
here in 1676
Below: Castle Stalker, Loch Linnhe*

Tour 13

Although never a separate legal entity, Fife earned the title 'Kingdom of Fife' through the influence of its ancient abbey in Dunfermline and later its medieval university in St Andrews. Cut off from the rest of the country by the great firths of the Forth and the Tay, it has a character that is very different from the rest of Scotland. This is most evident in its traditional architecture, especially the small white stone buildings with their pantiled roofs that are so common in the picturesque fishing villages of the East Neuk.

2/3 days – 177 miles (286km)

ARGYLL

Oban ● Easdale ● Kilmartin ● Crinan ● Lochgilphead
Crarae Garden ● Auchindrain ● Inveraray ● Loch Awe
Glen Coe ● Ballachulish ● Castle Stalker
Oban Sea Life Centre ● Loch Etive ● Oban

Oban's history as a fishing port goes back only as far as 1786, but the site of the ruined 14th-century *Dunollie Castle*, a stronghold of the Lords of Lorne, has been fortified since the 7th century. The town's most unusual feature is *McCaig's Folly*, built in the manner of Rome's Colosseum at the end of the 19th century to give work to the unemployed. It sits above the town with fine views towards the Firth of Lorne. Although most visitors come to Oban for the magnificent scenery or to take a ferry to the islands, the town has many attractions like factory visits round *Oban Glassworks*, *Oban Distillery* and *Highbank Pottery*, as well as *A World in Miniature*, an exhibition of miniature furniture and toys.

Dunstaffnage Castle stands a few miles north of Oban. This magnificent castle was erected in the 13th century and has massively thick walls. It was a MacDougall stronghold but was captured from them in 1308 by Robert the Bruce.

Almost 200 tartans exist in Scotland today, each one clearly attached to a particular clan

ⅈ Boswell House, Argyll Square

*Head south on the **A816**, then turn right at the **B844** which leads to Easdale (16 miles/ 26km).*

Easdale, Strathclyde

1 The village of Easdale lies on the island of Seil, connected to the mainland by the humped bridge known as the 'Bridge over the Atlantic'. The village shares its name with a little island just off shore which houses a **museum**.

Easdale was a slate quarrying centre and the rows of quarriers' houses look much as they did in the 19th century. The quarries reached below sea level and in 1881 a ferocious sea broke their walls and flooded the workings; no repairs could be made and the industry never recovered.

*Return along the **B844**, then turn right at the **A816** and follow this to Kilmartin, a total distance of 29 miles (47km).*

Kilmartin, Strathclyde

2 The area around the small village of Kilmartin has some of Scotland's most outstanding large **cairns**, forming a huge 'linear cemetery' that follows the Kilmartin Burn. West of the village is the massive Bronze Age **Glebe Cairn** and southwest of the village are the three **Nether Largie Cairns**. The cairns were used as tombs from around 5,000 years ago with bodies or cremated remains interred in stone-clad cells ('cists') within the cairns. A little further to the southwest lie the two **Temple Wood Stone Circles**.

Kilmartin Church's graveyard contains many celebrated sculptured gravestones, including the **Poltalloch Stones**, the gravestones of the Malcolm chiefs. Other large carved stones (the 'Kilmartin Crosses') can be seen inside the church.

The 16th-century fortified house known as **Carnassarie Castle** can be seen upon a hill just before the village is entered.

*Continue on the **A816**, then turn on to the **B8025** to meet the Crinan Canal. Turn right at the **B841** and follow it to Crinan.*

Crinan, Strathclyde

3 The **Crinan Canal** was opened in 1801 so boats could avoid the cruel seas around the Mull of Kintyre. This was a great boon to fishermen as the shortcut was only 8½ miles (14km) long compared to the sea route of 130 miles (200km). The advent of steamships dealt the canal a severe blow as they could manage the open sea, but it is still in use today and can be busy with pleasure craft.

*Return along the **B841** which follows the canal. Join the **A816** and follow it to Lochgilphead, 7 miles (11km).*

Fishing boats, car ferries and yachts make Oban harbour one of the most energetic in Scotland

Lochgilphead, Strathclyde

4 The town developed as an administrative centre for the region and also because of the trade brought by the canal, whose eastern terminus is at **Ardrishaig**, 2 miles (3km) to the south.

i Lochnell Street

*Leave by the **A83** for 14 miles (23km) to Crarae Garden.*

Crarae Garden, Strathclyde

5 The garden was founded in 1912 in a steep-sided gorge and today has a rich collection of rhododendrons, magnolias, azaleas and many other mature trees from around the world. The warmth of the Gulf Stream and an annual rainfall of 75 inches (190cm) help ensure that the garden delights visitors throughout the year, especially in early summer (for the rhododendrons) and in autumn.

*Continue on the **A83** for 5 miles (8km) to Auchindrain, just beyond the village of Furnace.*

Auchindrain, Strathclyde

6 Queen Victoria visited this little Highland township in 1875 and was impressed enough to record it in her diary. Today, the houses, barns, smiddy (blacksmith) and other buildings of this fascinating community have been preserved as an open air folk-life museum to show how people have lived here through the centuries.

*Continue on the **A83** for 6 miles (10km) to Inveraray.*

Inveraray, Strathclyde

7 This neat and well-planned village on Loch Fyne has been a royal burgh since 1648, but its 'modern' planning dates back to the middle of the 18th century, and the houses have been changed little in outward appearance since then.

The large **parish church** dominates the centre of the village and is sited in the middle of the main road. It was built at the turn of the 18th century with a central dividing wall so that services in Gaelic and English could be conducted simultaneously.

The fascinating **Inveraray Jail Museum** consists of the former courthouse (complete with a trial in progress) and two prisons. The older one was erected in 1820 as the Argyll County Prison and the newer one was built to 'modern' standards in 1849. The cells feature displays explaining the harshness of prison life and the appalling conditions the prisoners were kept in.

Near the jail are the 'lands', rows of houses reminiscent of some old Edinburgh houses. Neil Munro, author of the *Para Handy* tales, was born close by.

Inveraray Castle stands a short distance away from the village. The present building is mid-18th-century and replaces a castle built by Colin Campbell in about 1415. This is the home of the Dukes of Argyll, chiefs of Clan Campbell, and it has many exhibits relating to the clan's history.

i Front Street

*Leave by the **A819** and turn left at the **A85** for Loch Awe.*

The cone-topped towers of Inveraray Castle seem entirely appropriate to a Scottish scene

Loch Awe, Strathclyde

8 Loch Awe is dominated by the massive **Ben Cruachan**, a mountain with a pump storage hydroelectric power station inside it. Visits into the heart of the mountain start from the visitor centre (west along the A85).

At the head of the loch stands the imposing ruin of **Kilchurn Castle**, a Campbell stronghold built in the 15th and 17th centuries. It was abandoned in the 18th century and in 1879 a hurricane blew down the top of the tower that can be seen lying in the courtyard.

The intriguing **St Conan's Church** sits below the southeastern slopes of Ben Cruachan. This was started in 1881 and added to over the next 50 years. It has elaborate carvings, rich woodwork and a rare mixture of styles, including fragments from Iona Abbey.

*Return eastwards along the **A85**, then bear left at the **B8074** towards Bridge of Orchy. Turn left at the **A82** and follow it across Rannoch Moor to Glen Coe (36 miles/58km).*

Glen Coe, Highland

9 Glen Coe itself is regarded by many Scots as the country's finest glen and, no matter whether the sun is shining or the sky is black, it provides dramatic scenery that is difficult to better.

FOR HISTORY BUFFS

2 *Kilmartin, Strathclyde* **Dunadd** is a rocky promontory that rises steeply above the River Add, south of Kilmartin. This was the capital of the ancient Scots kingdom of Dalriada and the coronation site of the first Scottish kings, and was occupied intermittently between the 6th and 9th centuries. Rocky ramparts guard the summit where there is a flat rock with carvings of a foot and a boar

FOR CHILDREN

Oban, Strathclyde An animal-based attraction is the **Oban Rare Breeds Farm Park** with its collection of pigs, sheep and cattle.

7 *Inveraray, Strathclyde* **The Argyll Wildlife Park** near Inveraray boasts many animals including wildcats, badgers, wild boar and deer.

BACK TO NATURE

Oban, Strathclyde Oban Bay can be seen from the town's harbour. Look for common seals, black guillemots and eiders. There is a nature trail at nearby **Glen Nant** on the **B845**, south of Taynuilt. Look for wood warblers, redstarts and roe deer in the woodlands.

One of the most notable sights in many parts of western Scotland, particularly Argyll, is the rhododendron, a plant introduced in the 18th and 19th centuries. Its ability to colonise poor ground, together with its dense foliage that inhibits light reaching smaller plants, often makes people regard it more as a weed than an exotic plant to be nurtured.

SCENIC ROUTES

There can be few journeys in Scotland more exciting than that through Glen Coe. The route to it is over **Rannoch Moor**, a high peaty wasteland that was one of the last places to lose its ice at the close of the last Ice Age. The final approach is heralded by the **Buachaille Etive Mor**, (3,353 feet/1,022m), one of Scotland's most imposing mountains.

SPECIAL TO ...

Fresh seafood is a speciality of the region. Crabs, prawns and lobsters should be available in many restaurants and Loch Fyne is famous for its herrings. Herrings were once given the alternative name of '**Glasgow Magistrates**' as the quality of those sold in the city had to be approved by the magistrates. Indeed, the city used to give barrels of these delicious fish to people who rendered the city a great service!

The **visitor centre** near the foot of the glen has displays on the district and tells one of Scotland's most tragic stories, the Glencoe Massacre of February 1692. In 1691 William III offered a pardon to the warring clans if they took an oath of allegiance by 1 January 1692. The local MacDonald chief reluctantly went to Fort William just before the deadline to take the oath, only to be told he should go to Inveraray. He did so, but was a day late. The regiment in Glencoe was under the command of a Campbell and they were billeted with the MacDonalds for 10 days. A message was sent, which had the King's private approval, and at a given signal, without warning, the Campbells rose up and slaughtered 38 of their hosts, an atrocity which has never been forgotten. About 300 people escaped into the hills.

ⁱ NTS Visitor Centre

*Continue on the **A82** past the village of Glencoe for 4 miles (6km) to Ballachulish.*

Ballachulish, Highland

10 This was once Scotland's main slate producer and in the 1880s, the quarries' peak of production, 600 men produced 16 million slates a year. This ended in 1955 but the massive quarries can still be seen behind the houses. The tourist information centre has an interesting display on the life and work of the quarriers.

After passing under the **Ballachulish Bridge**, steps lead to a memorial to James Stewart who was hanged here in 1752 for the murder of Colin Campbell, a Government official. He was undoubtedly a scapegoat

convicted by a partisan court and Robert Louis Stevenson used this terrible miscarriage of justice in his novel *Kidnapped*.

*Continue on the **A82**, then follow the **A828** left to the village of Portnacroish for Castle Stalker.*

Castle Stalker, Strathclyde

11 This romantically set rectangular keep is perched on a low rocky platform at the mouth of Loch Laich. It was built by the Stewarts of Appin in the 13th century and in 1689, when it was in the possession of the Stewarts, it was exchanged for a meagre eight-oared galley during a drunken spree when the owner was not in full possession of his senses!

*Continue on the **A828** for 13 miles (21km) to the Oban Sea Life Centre, near Benderloch.*

Oban Sea Life Centre, Strathclyde

12 Scotland's west coast is famous for its important fishing grounds, so it is entirely appropriate to have the Sea Life Centre here. Crabs, lobsters, rays and a huge shoal of herring are just some of the exhibits on view. There are also seals and it provides sanctuary to abandoned seal pups.

*Continue on the **A828** to Connel where the road crosses the mouth of Loch Etive, a distance of (6 miles/10km).*

Loch Etive, Strathclyde

13 Just under the Connel Bridge are the unusual **Falls of Lora**, a tidal waterfall where the direction of the falls depends on whether the tide is going in or out.

To the east stands the village of Taynuilt. Its present-day peacefulness belies its past, as this was once one of Scotland's iron smelting centres and the impressive **Bonawe Furnace** has been conserved to show something of what an 18th-century ironworks looked like; however, you will have to forget the peace and quiet of the countryside to imagine all the dust, dirt and smoke it must have once produced.

*At Connel, join the **A85** and follow it westwards to return to Oban.*

Oban – Easdale **16 (26)**
Easdale – Kilmartin **29 (47)**
Kilmartin – Crinan **7 (11)**
Crinan – Lochgilphead **7 (11)**
Lochgilphead – Crarae Garden **14 (23)**
Crarae Garden – Auchindrain **5 (8)**
Auchindrain – Inveraray **6 (10)**
Inveraray – Loch Awe **15 (24)**
Loch Awe – Glen Coe **36 (58)**
Glen Coe – Ballachulish **4 (6)**
Ballachulish – Castle Stalker **14 (23)**
Castle Stalker – Oban Sea Life Centre **13 (21)**
Oban Sea Life Centre – Loch Etive **6 (10)**
Loch Etive – Oban **5 (8)**

The most infamous glen in Scotland, Glen Coe is sometimes referred to as the Glen of Weeping

RECOMMENDED WALKS

There are many easy forest walks in Argyll suitable for family outings, for example on the western shore of **Loch Awe**. The Crinan Canal towpath also provides pleasant walks, with lots to see when boats are passing through the locks.

9 *Glen Coe, Highland* Near Glen Coe, there are interesting stretches of the **West Highland Way**, such as the **Devil's Staircase**. The **Lost Valley** in Glen Coe is another good walk, but needs a bit of scrambling experience. Advice on walks in Glen Coe can be obtained from the NTS Visitor Centre.

2 days – 132 miles (213km)

'DOON THE WATTER'

Paisley ● Dumbarton ● Helensburgh ● Arrochar
Lochgoilhead ● Loch Fyne ● Tighnabruaich ● Dunoon
Gourock ● Kilbarchan ● Paisley

Paisley grew up around its *abbey*, founded in 1163. Only a few parts of the original building survived an English attack in 1307 during the Wars of Independence, and most of the structure seen today dates from rebuilding which took place in the middle of the 15th century. The town's most famous products are Paisley shawls, featuring the distinctive teardrop-shaped Paisley Pattern. The *Museum and Art Gallery* in High Street has a fine collection of shawls, as well as displays on local history. The *Sma' Shot Cottages* feature a restored artisan's house of the Victorian era, an 18th-century weaver's loom and a fully furnished loom shop. One rather fascinating institution near the museum is the *Coats Observatory*, which has been collecting astronomical and meteorological data since 1882.

An astronomically inspired stained glass window in the Coats Observatory, Paisley, bearing the portrait of the building's founder, Thomas Coats, a Scottish industrialist born in the town

ℹ Town Hall, Abbey Close

Leave Paisley on the A726 (to Greenock and Erskine Bridge). Join the M8 and head towards Greenock, then take the M898/ A898 to the Erskine Bridge (toll) over the River Clyde. Head west along the A82 (towards Crianlarich) then bear left on to the A814 (17 miles/27km).

Dumbarton, Strathclyde

1 A modern industrial town owing its historic importance to its prominent position on the northern shore of the River Clyde, Dumbarton was the capital of the ancient kingdom of Strathclyde and has had a royal castle since medieval times. **Dumbarton Castle** stands on Dumbarton Rock overlooking the river and much of the present fortification dates from the 16th to 18th centuries. The hilltop behind the castle gives a superb view of the area.

Dumbarton is now an important whisky distilling centre but it used to have a flourishing shipbuilding industry. Although few ships are built on the Clyde these days, one important structure that remains is the **Denny Tank** which has been preserved by the **Scottish Maritime Museum**. This was used for experiments; models of proposed ships were towed along the 330-foot (100m) tank in order to show how the full size ship might perform at sea.

ℹ Milton A82 northbound

Leave Dumbarton by the A814 and follow it along the coast for 8 miles (13km) to Helensburgh.

The river port of Dumbarton, one of many towns on the Clyde to suffer during the decline of the shipbuilding industry

Helensburgh, Strathclyde

2 Helensburgh's grand architecture dates back to the late 18th century when it was built as a planned dormitory town for Glasgow, to which it was connected by regular sailings. The town's long promenade gives a pleasant walk and by the seafront is a tall granite obelisk commemorating Henry Bell, designer of the world's first sea-going steamship, *The Comet*.

The recent revival in interest in the work of the outstanding Scottish architect and designer Charles Rennie Mackintosh makes a trip to **Hill House** one of the town's main attractions. This mansion was built at the beginning of the 20th century for the publisher Walter Blackie and remains an outstanding example of modern Scottish domestic architecture. The exterior design and the household furnishings reflect his individual style.

John Logie Baird, pioneer of television, came from Helensburgh and a memorial bust to him is in the town's **Hermitage Park**.

After leaving Helensburgh, the route passes the huge complex of the **Clyde Submarine Base**.

i Clock Tower, The Pier

> *Continue along the A814 for 17 miles (27km) to Arrochar.*

Arrochar, Strathclyde

3 The little village of Arrochar sits at the head of Loch Long and below the hills often referred to as the 'Arrochar Alps'. These rise steeply from the shore and provide wonderful walking and climbing, especially 2,891-foot (881m) Ben Arthur, usually known as **The Cobbler**.

Loch Long has been associated with seafarers for many centuries. The most notable naval exploit was in 1263 when the Viking King Haakon landed at Arrochar. He had his boats hauled 1½ miles (2km) over the strip of

Hand-woven tartans maintain the traditions of the cottage industry in the village of Kilbarchan

land to Tarbet and then sailed over Loch Lomond to attack inland settlements!

To the west of Arrochar, the A83 climbs steeply up Glen Croe to the well-named stopping place, the '**Rest and be thankful**' which is at an altitude of 803 feet (245m). Below this can be seen the earlier military road which was built after the 1745 Jacobite uprising in order to 'pacify' the Highlands.

> *Leave Arrochar on the A83 to Campbeltown. Turn left at the Rest and be thankful on to the B828, then join the B839 to reach Lochgoilhead.*

Lochgoilhead, Strathclyde

4 Set at the head of Loch Goil, this village is popular with visitors seeking good walking and sailing. Beside the village is the **European Sheep and Wool Centre**, part of a leisure complex

SPECIAL TO...

The development of steamships in the 19th century led to the 'discovery' of Cowal by visitors keen to go 'Doon the Watter' (the River Clyde) from Glasgow to the smoke-free countryside. Many wealthy Glasgow merchants built villas in the Cowal villages and decanted their families there during the summer months.

Cruising on the Clyde is now an increasingly popular pastime and cruises from places such as Dunoon and Tighnabruaich are available. One ship to look out for around Cowal is the PS *Waverley*, the world's last sea-going paddle steamer. It is based in Glasgow and operates many summer cruises, calling at piers on both sides of the Firth of Clyde.

SCENIC ROUTES

The nicest part of this tour is on the **A8003**, just after Tighnabruaich when the narrows of the **Kyles of Bute** are seen. If you are lucky you may see a ship negotiating the passage past the **Burnt Islands**. The true narrows are opposite the little settlement of **Colintraive**, whose name means 'strait of swimming', as cattle drovers used to swim their beasts across here.

FOR HISTORY BUFFS

7 *Dunoon, Strathclyde* Eight miles (13km) south of Dunoon stand the ruins of 15th-century **Castle Toward**. This was a stronghold of the Lamont clan, but in 1646 it was surrounded by a force of Campbells. Although the Lamonts accepted and signed a truce they were seized and taken to Dunoon where they were summarily executed and their bodies thrown into mass graves. This bloody act is commemorated by a memorial on Tom-a-Mhoid Road near Castle Hill.

that offers various sports, including curling in the winter.

Five miles (8km) down the western shore of the loch stands the gaunt ruin of **Carrick Castle**, destroyed by fire in 1685. The structure dates at least from the 15th century and was probably used by James IV when he came to Cowal to hunt wild boar. (Britain's last wild boar was killed in Cowal around 1690.)

*Leave Lochgoilhead by the **B839** and follow this to the shore of Loch Fyne. Turn left on to the **A815** just before the shore (9 miles/15km).*

Loch Fyne, Strathclyde

5 This long sea loch is set among beautiful ranges of green-clad mountains. Apart from the little village of Strachur, the district's settlements are small and scattered and many of the houses are used as retirement homes.

South of Strachur stands **Castle Lachlan**, home of the chief of the MacLachlans. During the Clearances the local people were moved out of their homes and settled in the village of Newton which the chief built between the castle and Strachur. This is now a sleepy hamlet, and many homes are used only at weekends.

The 18th-century Clearances, when landowners moved thousands of people off the land to make way for more profitable sheep farming, led to depopulation of the area. However, the importance of sheep has dimi-'nished greatly and much of the poorer land has been given over to extensive conifer plantations.

*Follow the **A815** to Strachur. Keep to the lochside by joining the **A886** and later bear right on to the **B8000** to Kilfinan. Follow this to Tighnabruaich.*

Tighnabruaich, Strathclyde

6 Both Tighnabruaich and neighbouring Kames grew during the heyday of steamship navigation on the Clyde and the Victorian villas date from this time. This is a popular sailing centre and many yachts, large and small, can be seen in the narrow waterways around the northern coast of Bute. Just north of Tighnabruaich is one of Scotland's most famous viewpoints – across the narrow strait known as the Kyles of Bute.

*Leave Tighnabruaich by the **A8003**. Turn right at the **A886** and then left at the **B836**. Turn right when the **A815** is met for Dunoon, a distance of 17 miles (27km).*

Dunoon, Strathclyde

7 Dunoon has built up a reputation as one of the most popular stopping places for people sailing 'Doon the Watter' and its picturesque pierhead buildings have welcomed countless visitors. As befits a seaside resort, it has a long **promenade** and colourful **Castle Gardens**.

Near the pier stands a statue of Robert Burns' 'Highland Mary' who was born in the town. This was Mary Campbell, who was betrothed to Burns but died. Burns tried hard to cover up their relationship, probably because it complicated his life with his future wife, Jean Armour. A **castle**, which was razed in 1685, stood on the high ground behind the statue and this viewpoint provides a fine outlook over the busy Clyde.

Dunoon is world famous for its **Cowal Highland Gathering** which takes place on the last Friday and Saturday in August. The Gathering was started in the 1890s and today it attracts competitors from many countries as it hosts the **World Highland**

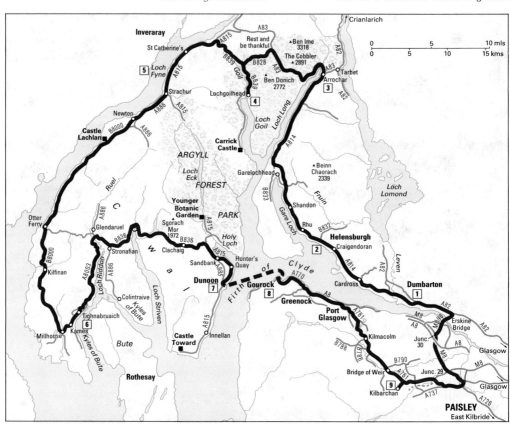

Dancing Championships. Pipe bands from near and far compete at the Gathering and some 20,000 visitors may throng the main street watching the bands marching through the town.

The **Younger Botanic Garden** is at Benmore, just 7 miles (11km) north of Dunoon on the **A815**. This outstanding garden is an outstation of Edinburgh's Royal Botanic Garden; it has a magnificent collection of rhododendrons and an avenue of tall redwoods, planted in 1863.

i 7 Alexandra Parade

*Take the Caledonian MacBrayne ferry from Dunoon to Gourock. Alternatively, take the Western Ferries' ferry from Hunter's Quay (just north of Dunoon) to a point a little southwest of Gourock; then head towards Gourock on the **A770**.*

Gourock, Strathclyde

8 Gourock is a pleasant coastal town that boasts excellent views of the Clyde. Perhaps the best view is from **Lyle Hill** which stands above the southeastern side of Gourock Bay. On top of the hill is a monument in the form of a Cross of Lorraine commemorating Free French sailors who sailed from here and died during World War II's Battle of the Atlantic.

To the east of Gourock are the industrial towns of Greenock and Port Glasgow. **Greenock** was a shipbuilding centre and once an important embarkation point for emigrants leaving Scotland for new lives in North America or Australasia. The town's most famous son was the engineer James Watt, whose invention of the condensing steam engine, the first efficient use of steam power, paved the way for the Industrial Revolution. The privateer and pirate Captain Kidd may also have come from Greenock, but would any town want to claim him as one of their own?

Unceasingly peaceful surroundings envelop the visitor at the Younger Botanic Garden, Benmore. This large-scale woodland garden is particularly colourful in late spring to early summer

Port Glasgow gained its present name in 1688 when it became the city's port as ships could not progress further upstream. Its previous name was Newark and its 16th-century castle stands by the shore, dominated these days by all the surrounding industrial buildings.

*Leave Gourock by the coastal road (the **A770** which joins the **A8** at Greenock) and bear right on to the **A761** to Bridge of Weir, via Kilmacolm. After Bridge of Weir, continue on the **A761** for 1½ miles (2½km) after the local railway station, then turn sharp right at a signposted minor road to Kilbarchan.*

Kilbarchan, Strathclyde

9 In the 18th century the village of Kilbarchan was an important centre where wool, linen and cotton were hand woven. A weaver's cottage of 1723 has been preserved at **The Cross** by the NTS. This continued to be used for weaving until 1940 and it has a 200-year-old loom on which demonstrations are given.

*Rejoin the **A761** (to Paisley, via Linwood), then turn left on to the **A737** to return to Paisley, 6 miles (10km).*

Paisley – Dumbarton 17 (27)
Dumbarton – Helensburgh 8 (13)
Helensburgh – Arrochar 17 (27)
Arrochar – Lochgoilhead 13 (21)
Lochgoilhead – Loch Fyne 9 (15)
Loch Fyne – Tighnabruaich 29 (47)
Tighnabruaich – Dunoon 17 (27)
Dunoon – Gourock ferry
Gourock – Kilbarchan 16 (26)
Kilbarchan – Paisley 6 (10)

FOR CHILDREN

Cowal is an area for outdoor activities with sailing at Tighnabruaich and ponytrekking at Lochgoilhead and Innellan (south of Dunoon). As a wet-weather alternative, there are swimming pools in Dunoon and Lochgoilhead.

BACK TO NATURE

The sea lochs around Cowal are home to many seabirds including gulls, cormorants and ducks. Keep a sharp look out for seals from the shore of Loch Fyne. Of all Cowal's lochs, Loch Striven is probably the quietest and least touched by agriculture.

RECOMMENDED WALKS

Serious walkers will head for the **Arrochar Alps**, but experience is needed before these hills are tackled. There are many walks of varying grades in the **Argyll Forest Park** which lies in the area of lochs Long, Goil and Eck. Information can be obtained from tourist information centres.

ROB ROY COUNTRY

Glasgow • Gartocharn • Luss • Killin • Kenmore
Aberfeldy • Crieff • Lochearnhead • Callander
Loch Katrine • Aberfoyle • Glasgow

Glasgow, the industrial centre of Scotland, stands on the banks of the River Clyde. Few medieval buildings remain, the main ones being the 13th-century *cathedral* and the nearby *Provand's Lordship*, Glasgow's oldest house, which was built around 1471. Glasgow's museums and galleries are among Britain's finest, especially the *Burrell Collection*, the *Art Galleries and Museum* and the *Transport Museum*. Slightly less well-known, in Glasgow University, are the *Hunterian Museum* and *Hunterian Art Gallery*, home of the *Whistler Collection*. Part of the gallery is a replica of the *Charles Rennie Mackintosh House*. The *People's Palace* (in Glasgow Green), has a wonderful collection of displays depicting the lives of Glaswegians.

The city is well endowed with green spaces with *Kelvingrove Park*, the *Botanic Gardens* and *Pollok Park* among the most popular.

A thriving village community exists behind Aberfoyle's tourist frontings

ℹ 35 St Vincent Place

*Leave by the **A81**, then the **A809** and turn left at the **A811** to reach Gartocharn (20 miles/32km).*

Gartocharn, Strathclyde

1 This small village gives a good introduction to Scotland's most-loved loch, **Loch Lomond**. Although Gartocharn doesn't actually sit on the lochside, there is a superb view of it from the little hill behind, **Duncryne**. For little effort, this is a vantage point that gives views towards the loch, 3,194-foot (974m) Ben Lomond on the east shore and the Luss Hills, which rise from the western shore.

The area around the loch was one of the last places to lose its glaciers at the end of the last Ice Age and the smooth, U-shaped glacial valleys in the Luss Hills are obvious features of this type of landscape. The careful observer will notice a change between this glacially eroded Highland landscape and the smoothly sculpted hillocks around Gartocharn's farmland. This change indicates the geological divide between the Highlands and the Lowlands.

Further along the road, at Balloch, there are cruises available on the loch and pleasant walks in the **Balloch Castle Country Park**.

ℹ Balloch Road

*Continue on the **A811** and turn right at the **A82**. Follow this northwards, turning off on to an unclassified road where signposted to Luss, a distance of 12 miles (19km).*

A yacht festooned corner of Loch Lomond, seen from Balhana, near Drymen

SCENIC ROUTES

Much of the route is through fine scenery, with perhaps the nicest parts being along the shores of lochs Lomond and Tay for views of the lochs and their mountains. Another fine stretch is through the pretty **Sma' Glen** (between Aberfeldy and Crieff) where the River Almond winds its way through the hills.

Luss, Strathclyde

2 The delightful little lochside village of Luss, made famous by the television programme *Take the High Road*, has many exceptionally picturesque cottages. Wordsworth and his sister visited Luss in 1803, as did Coleridge.

Further north, a ferry operates from Inverbeg across the loch to Rowardennan.

*Rejoin and continue on the **A82**, then turn right on to the **A85** at Crianlarich. Turn left at the **A827** to Killin (39 miles/63km).*

Killin, Central

3 Killin is a popular centre with hill walkers as there are so many fine hills in the district, the best known of which is Ben Lawers, at 3,984 feet (1,214m). The NTS has established a **visitor centre** on the western flank of the mountain.

The River Dochart flows past the village before debouching into Loch Tay and on its way tumbles over the wide **Falls of Dochart**, which are quite fearsome when the river is in spate.

i Main Street

*Continue on the **A827** for 17 miles (27km) to Kenmore.*

Kenmore, Tayside

4 On the shores of Loch Tay, Kenmore has been developed as a small resort and watersports centre. Beside the village is the ornamental gateway to 19th-century **Taymouth** Castle (private), which stands in fine parkland, part of which is now used as a golf course.

To the north lies the quiet settlement of **Fortingall**, reputedly the birthplace of Pontius Pilate, which has several roadside thatched cottages. A yew tree in the churchyard is said to be over 3,000 years old.

*Continue on the **A827** for 6 miles (10km) to Aberfeldy.*

Aberfeldy, Tayside

5 This pleasant touring centre stands beside the splendidly ornate **bridge** which General George Wade built in 1733 at this important crossing of the River Tay. Wade was responsible for some 250 miles (400km) of military roads in the Highlands between 1726 and 1735, as part of the Government's attempt to gain control over the region. This network included 40 stone bridges, of which this is the best known, and at the time it was the only bridge over the Tay.

The **Black Watch Memorial**, which stands quite close to the bridge, was erected in 1887. The regiment was enrolled into the British Army in 1739 and took its name from the men's dark tartan, chosen to differentiate them from the Guardsmen or Red Soldiers.

Aberfeldy lies in a belt of good agricultural land and the **water mill** is one enduring reminder of how the local grain was processed. This was originally built in 1825 and has been restored to allow it to produce stone-ground oatmeal.

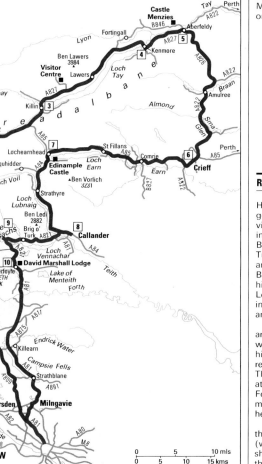

FOR HISTORY BUFFS

7 *Lochearnhead, Central* The peaceful little settlement of **Balquhidder**, by Loch Voil, was where Rob Roy died. He is buried in the local churchyard.

10 *Aberfoyle, Central* To the east of Aberfoyle lies the Lake of Menteith, Scotland's only 'lake', apart from the artificial Pressmennan lake. On one of the lake's islands, Inchmahome, stands the **Priory of Inchmahome**, founded in 1238. Mary, Queen of Scots, was sent to the island at the age of five, prior to sailing to France in 1547. The island can be reached by ferry from the nearby Port of Menteith.

A steamer trip on the Sir Walter Scott *provides a splendid panoramic view of Loch Katrine and its rugged scenery*

To the northwest of the village, at **Weem**, stands **Castle Menzies**, home of the chief of Clan Menzies. The present castle, Z-shaped in plan, was built in the 1570s, and has been restored by the Clan Society.

ⓘ 8 Dunkeld Street

*Leave by the **A826**, then turn right at the **A822**. Turn right at the **A85** and follow this into Crieff.*

Crieff, Tayside

6 Crieff is a traditional Highland resort and one that offers much to the casual walker or the visitor wanting a base to explore the countryside.

The **Weavers' House and Highland Tryst Museum** has demonstrations of the skills of local hand-loom weavers. The local **Glenturret Distillery**, founded in 1775, has a visitor centre and tours round the premises.

West of Crieff, on the A85, is **Comrie**, the home of the only museum of tartan in the world.

ⓘ The Square

*Continue on the **A85** for 19 miles (31km) to Lochearnhead.*

Lochearnhead, Central

7 Lochearnhead, sitting at the western end of Loch Earn, was developed when the railway was built through **Glen Ogle**. The line's route can be followed through the glen and it is a sobering experience to see the massive boulders that have tumbled down the hillside and must have threatened the trains that chugged northwards up the steep incline.

Near the village, and where the Burn of Ample meets the loch, stands

Edinample Castle which was built in 1630.

*Leave by the **A84** and follow it for 14 miles (23km) to Callander.*

Callander, Central

8 This is one of Central Scotland's busiest little resorts as it is a favourite stopping place for many visitors.

The town stands by the banks of the River Teith and has many good walks near by. Serious walkers head for **Ben Ledi**, which dominates the local scenery at 2,882 feet (879m), or the rather higher **Ben Vorlich**, at 3,231 feet (985m) which stands between Callander and Loch Earn.

Much of the town was laid out in the 18th century as a planned village with its centre at Ancaster Square which now houses the **Rob Roy and Trossachs Visitor Centre**. Rob Roy MacGregor (1671–1734) was a most intriguing character and the hero of Sir Walter Scott's novel *Rob Roy*. The story of Rob Roy's life is intertwined with legend and Scott's artistic licence. However, he did represent the last flings of Gaeldom against the encroaching 'civilisation' of the Highlands by English and lowland Scottish 'culture' as well as naked economic and political might. At the end of the 17th century the king, William of Orange, was determined to subdue the Highlanders and even took the step of proscribing the name MacGregor. Rob Roy then used his mother's clan name of Campbell and allied himself with his kinsman, the Duke of Argyll, in feuds with the Duke of Montrose. When Montrose chased him out of his home, he turned his hand from cattle dealing to reiving (cattle raiding), earning a reputation as the Scots equivalent of Robin Hood, stealing from the rich landowners and giving the money to destitute Highlanders.

ⓘ Ancaster Square

*Return along the **A84** and then turn left at the **A821**. After passing the Trossachs Hotel, follow the signs (right) to Loch Katrine.*

Loch Katrine, Central

9 The loch lies in the heart of the area known as the Trossachs, though the name is properly given to the little pass between lochs Achray and Katrine. Its fame as a beauty spot stemmed from Sir Walter Scott's description of it in the poem *The Lady of the Lake*; Dorothy Wordsworth and others also described its charms. The road between it and Aberfoyle is known as the **Duke's Pass**, as it was built in the 19th century by the Duke of Montrose to cater for the growing number of visitors coming to this part of the country, drawn here by Scott's work.

The loch is one of the main sources of Glasgow's water and the 1855 scheme to pipe this very pure water the 35 miles (56km) to the city was a massive feat of civil engineering. Today, visitors can cruise on the *Sir Walter Scott* across the loch and under the slopes of **Ben Venue**.

*Return to the **A821** and turn right. Follow the **A821** to Aberfoyle, 7 miles (11km).*

Aberfoyle, Central

10 Aberfoyle is a tourist centre sitting by the River Forth and seemingly hemmed in by a very large conifer plantation, much of it in the **Queen Elizabeth Forest Park**. The 'Clachan at Aberfoyle' was one of the settings used by Scott in *Rob Roy* (a clachan is Scots for a small village), and the name of the local hotel, the Baillie Nicol Jarvie, celebrates one of the novel's characters.

i Main Street

*Continue on the **A821** and then the **A81**. Follow this back to Glasgow (29 miles/47km).*

Glasgow – Gartocharn **20 (32)**
Gartocharn – Luss **12 (19)**
Luss – Killin **39 (63)**
Killin – Kenmore **17 (27)**
Kenmore – Aberfeldy **6 (10)**
Aberfeldy – Crieff **23 (37)**
Crieff – Lochearnhead **19 (31)**
Lochearnhead – Callander **14 (23)**
Callander – Loch Katrine **10 (16)**
Loch Katrine – Aberfoyle **7 (11)**
Aberfoyle – Glasgow **29 (47)**

This gently tumbling waterfall graces the River Dochart at Killin, above Loch Tay. Seen in spate, the fall presents a dramatically different picture. The Ben Lawers range is obvious in the distance

SPECIAL TO...

Every visitor to Scotland wants to see Highland cattle, those fierce-looking, shaggy beasts with long curved horns. In reality, these lovely creatures turn out to be very docile and more interested in eating than worrying about hordes of people. They can be seen in a number of localities, but keep a special lookout for them north of Loch Lomond and at the western end of Loch Tay.

1/2 days – 91 miles (148km)

ABBEYS, BATTLEFIELDS & CASTLES

FIRE POINT

Stirling ● Causewayhead ● Dunblane ● Dollar ● Culross
Dunfermline ● Blackness ● Linlithgow ● Bo'ness
Bannockburn ● Stirling

Stirling must rank as one of Scotland's nicest towns. It has a pleasant blend of historic buildings and the advantages of an important cultural and administrative centre. The status of the town was greatly enhanced by the establishment, in 1967, of the University of Stirling which is situated at Bridge of Allan.

Stirling Castle, a royal stronghold since the 12th century, has had a commanding position on the eastern route into the Highlands for many centuries, and saw two great battles during the Wars of Independence – in 1297 at Stirling Bridge and in 1314 at Bannockburn.

Other fine buildings include the *Argyll Lodging, Mar's Wark, Cowane's Hospital* (the Guildhall), the *Church of the Holy Rude* and the *Tolbooth.* The medieval *Stirling Old Bridge,* which spans the Forth, can be seen from the esplanade and is worth walking to.

FOR CHILDREN

Stirling, Central The **Blair Drummond Safari and Leisure Park** is to be found to the northwest of Stirling, on the flat agricultural land of the Carse of Stirling. The most fascinating part of the park is the drive round the main enclosure where you can observe such animals as lions, bison, zebra and deer at very close quarters; don't be surprised if monkeys clamber all over your car!

The halcyon days of steam are re-created by the Bo'ness and Kinneil Railway, with the aid of relocated historic railway buildings

i 41 Dumbarton Road

*Leave by the **A9** and follow it for 1 mile (2km) to Causewayhead.*

Causewayhead, Central

1 This small village is dominated by the **Abbey Craig** upon which is perched the 220-foot (67m) high **Wallace Monument**, erected in tribute to Sir William Wallace, victor of the Battle of Stirling Bridge. The top of the monument gives an outstanding view of the district.

Close by in a meander of the Forth stands the ruined **Cambuskenneth Abbey**, founded around 1147.

*Continue on the **A9**. Just before Dunblane, turn right at a roundabout at the end of the **M9** and follow the **B8033**. Take a signposted road on the left into the village, 5 miles (8km).*

Dunblane, Central

2 The **cathedral**, which is situated near the Allan Water, was founded around 1150 and its presence raises the status of the village to that of a small city.

To the west lies the quiet village of **Doune**, at various times a droving centre and a pistol-making centre. The main attractions today are the fine medieval **castle** and the collection of

A large part of Stirling Castle dates from the 15th and 16th centuries, when it became a favourite residence of the royal family

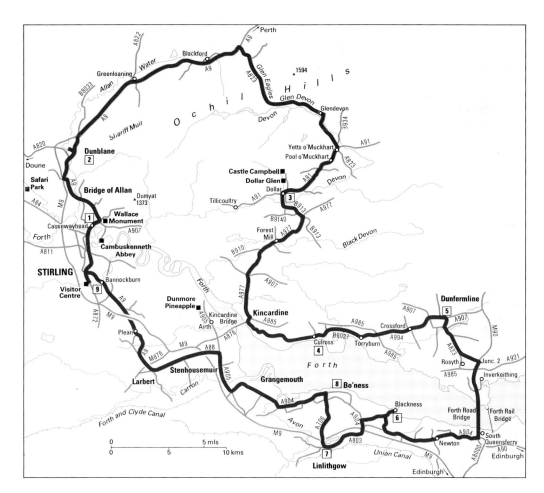

rare vehicles in the Motor Museum, including the world's second oldest Rolls Royce.

ⓘ Stirling Road, Dunblane

*Return to the **B8033** and turn left. Join the **A9** and head northeast. Turn right at the **A823**, then right at the **A91** in order to enter Dollar, a distance of 23 miles (37km).*

Dollar, Central

3 This neat little town lies in a sheltered position at the foot of the Ochil Hills and one of its chief attractions is the wooded Dollar Glen, through which a path runs to **Castle Campbell**. This stands on a promontory overlooking the confluence of two streams, intriguingly named the Burn of Sorrow and the Burn of Care. Until 1490 it was called Castle Glume, hence it is sometimes referred to as the 'castle of gloom'.

Dollar is one of the Hillfoot towns, small mill towns which gained prosperity through the woollen industry. A **mill trail** links these communities and guides visitors through the district. Tillicoultry's **Clock Mill Heritage Centre** is the focal point of this trail and it has displays explaining the history of the local woollen industry.

ⓘ Clock Mill, Upper Mill Street, Tillicoultry

*Leave by the **B913** and turn right at the **A977**. Turn right at the **A876**, heading towards Kincardine Bridge, turn left just before and follow an unclassified road along the coast to Culross, a distance of 13 miles (21km).*

Culross, Fife

4 Culross, frozen in time, is possibly Scotland's most remarkable town. During the 16th and 17th centuries, it prospered by trading in coal and salt with ports across the North Sea, but when this failed, the town declined. Fortunately it never really changed during the industrial development of the succeeding centuries, so although it is quite small it preserves many of the features that have been lost in other ancient towns. The NTS has played a major part in conserving this unique place, especially through its 'Little Houses Scheme', and today numerous buildings can be visited, whisking you back through the centuries. Cobbled streets and white-painted buildings with pantiled roofs help to produce an air that is so very different from any other Scottish town and the virtual completeness of the medieval character of Culross has attracted many television and film companies to locations here.

The town's main building, the **Palace**, was never in fact a royal mansion at all, but the home of the local laird, George Bruce, and was originally built between 1597 and 1611. The title deeds describe it as 'the Palace of Great Lodging in the Sand Haven of Culross'. Among the other fascinating buildings here, visitors should look out for the **Town House**, the **Study**, the **House of the Evil Eye** and the abbey.

*Continue on the unclassified road, then turn right at the **B9037**. Join the **A994** which leads to Dunfermline (7 miles/11km).*

BACK TO NATURE

As Scotland's ice-caps receded at the end of the last Ice Age, the reduction of the great weight of ice made the land rise slowly. This happened gradually and the sea level slowly fell to its present position. Areas such as the low-lying 'carselands' around Stirling had peat bogs growing in this 'new' land and these remained undrained until the agricultural improvements of the late 18th century. The **Blairdrummond Moss** remained virtually untouched until 1767 when the layers of peat were stripped off; extensive draining, ploughing and liming have now led to the establishment of a rich stretch of agricultural land.

SCENIC ROUTES

The journey through the picturesque **Glen Eagles** and **Glen Devon** is the most scenic part of the tour, with the road making its way through the heart of the Ochils. Two misconceptions about Glen Eagles should be explained; firstly, the name means 'churches' and not 'eagles' and secondly, the well-known golfing hotel of Gleneagles is not here but near Auchterarder.

SPECIAL TO...

There can be few bridges in the world as distinctive in appearance as the **Forth Rail Bridge**, which can be seen from so many places on this route. This was the world's first really major structure to be made entirely of steel and it took eight years, from 1883 to 1890, to erect. It is over 1½ miles (2.5km) long and from mid-winter to mid-summer its length expands by about three feet (1m)!

Dunfermline, Fife

5 Dunfermline was built around the substantial Benedictine abbey which was constructed in the 12th century. Apart from the Abbey Church, there are the ruins of the monastery's domestic buildings and the palace, which was often used as the abbey's guest house. The abbey church was a favoured place with the Scottish kings and it superseded Iona as their place of burial. The great warrior, King Robert the Bruce, was buried here but it was only in 1818 that this fact was known for certain. During some restoration work, a skeleton, dressed in what may have been royal robes, was discovered and it was noticed that the breast bone had been sawn in order to remove one of the organs. This would have been in accordance with Bruce's deathbed wish in 1329 that upon his death his heart be removed and taken to the Holy Land as his way of making up for not taking part in the Crusades. His heart was buried in Melrose Abbey.

Opposite the door of the abbey church is the entrance to the extensive and pleasant **Pittencrieff Park**. Within the grounds is Pittencrieff House, built in the 17th century. There is a small **museum** of local history with an art gallery and a costume exhibition here.

Just by the edge of the park stands the weaver's cottage where Andrew Carnegie was born in 1835. In 1848 his family emigrated to the United States where he made his massive fortune in the steel industry. He then began to give much of his wealth away, buying Pittencrieff Park for the town and establishing trusts that endowed libraries and other public enterprises. The cottage is now the location of the **Andrew Carnegie Birthplace Museum**.

The Regency-style grandeur of the House of the Binns, 4 miles (6km) east of Linlithgow. The 15th-century house, remodelled in the 17th, has elaborately moulded plaster ceilings dating from 1630

[i] Abbot House, Maygate

Leave by the A823 and the A823M, then join the M90 to cross the Forth Road Bridge (toll). Turn right on to the A904, then left and right as signed to Blackness (14 miles/23km).

Blackness, Lothian

6 The little village of Blackness, once an important seaport, is dominated by the great fortress of **Blackness Castle**. This was built to protect the port which was the harbour for the great royal palace at Linlithgow. Construction of the castle started as a fairly small affair in the 15th century, but with later technical improvements in artillery it became necessary to strengthen it to withstand massive sea-borne attacks. After the Union with England in 1707, it was one of the four castles in Scotland to be left fortified.

Return until the A904 is met. Turn left on to the A904 and then follow the A803 to Linlithgow, a distance of 5 miles (8km).

Linlithgow, Lothian

7 The history of the town is intimately interwoven with that of the **palace**, the birthplace of Mary, Queen of Scots, and one of the country's most important historical buildings. There was some form of royal residence here in the 14th century, but the palace was not started until the early 16th century. It was certainly a substantial and well-defended building, occupying an attractive site overlooking Linlithgow Loch. Everything seems to have been constructed to a grand scale, especially the enormous fireplaces and the ornate fountain that stands in the quadrangle in the heart of the building.

Linlithgow has a number of other fine buildings and monuments sited near the palace or on the main street and these include the **Church of St Michael**, the **Burgh Halls** and the **Cross Well**.

The **Union Canal**, which joined the Forth and Clyde Canal to the heart of Edinburgh, runs along the town's outskirts. This was originally built to bring coal from Lanarkshire into the capital. Work on the canal started in 1818 and it opened in 1822, finally closing in 1965. There is a **canal museum** at the Manse Road Basin and cruises on the waterway are available.

ⓘ Burgh Halls, The Cross

*Leave by the **A706** for 3 miles (5km) to Bo'ness.*

Bo'ness, Central

8 This long-established industrial town was once the third most important seaport in Scotland until the building of the Forth and Clyde Canal and the establishment of the major port at Grangemouth put it into decline. Bo'ness' past has included such diverse enterprises as potteries, salt pans, iron foundries and coal mines and it is most appropriate that the town's visitor facilities have taken advantage of this rich industrial legacy. It is possible to walk through the tunnels of the **Birkhill Clay Mine** and visit **Hamilton's Cottage**, a small cottage of the 1920s. The **Bo'ness and Kinneil Railway** operates steam trains on its 3½-mile (6km) track that runs along the foreshore.

*Leave by the **A904** and turn right at the **A905**. Turn left at the **A88** and right at the **A9**. Continue on this road towards Stirling and turn left at the **A872** to reach the NTS Visitor Centre at Bannockburn, 18 miles (29km).*

The Forth Rail Bridge owes its striking appearance to an Admiralty decree that there should be adequate headroom and manoeuvring space for warships

Bannockburn, Central

9 The Battle of Bannockburn in 1314 was one of the most important events in the fight for Scottish independence. At the time, an English force held Stirling Castle and was being besieged by Robert the Bruce's brother. The English army, led by their king, came north to relieve the castle and a pitched battle took place here. The Scots army, led by Bruce, eventually routed the enemy after they took fright at seeing a 'new' army (in reality, the Scots camp followers) come over the Gillies Hill.

The story of the battle and the history of that period is explained in the NTS's **Visitor Centre** and the impressive memorial to the battle is in the form of a bronze equestrian statue of Bruce erected where his command post is thought to have been positioned.

ⓘ NTS Visitor Centre

*Return along the **A872** and turn left at the **B8051** for the drive back to Stirling.*

Stirling – Causewayhead **1 (2)**
Causewayhead – Dunblane **5 (8)**
Dunblane – Dollar **23 (37)**
Dollar – Culross **13 (21)**
Culross – Dunfermline **7 (11)**
Dunfermline – Blackness **14 (23)**
Blackness – Linlithgow **5 (8)**
Linlithgow – Bo'ness **3 (5)**
Bo'ness – Bannockburn **18 (29)**
Bannockburn – Stirling **2 (4)**

FOR HISTORY BUFFS

Stirling, Central In Dunmore Park, southeast of Stirling on the **A905**, is a curious garden retreat called the **Dunmore Pineapple**, with a pineapple-shaped roof. It was part of an extensive walled garden at Dunmore Park and was built in 1761 by the Earl of Dunmore on his return from holding the governorship of Jamaica. It has been restored by the NTS and can be rented as a holiday home.

RECOMMENDED WALKS

The 1,373-foot (418m) summit of **Dumyat**, the most prominent hill at the western end of the Ochils offers a pleasant walk and a superb viewpoint. The most straightforward route to it is from the west, from near Bridge of Allan's reservoir. The Battle of Sheriffmuir was fought on the moor some way behind the hill in 1715.

1/2 days – 120 miles (192km)

RASPBERRY FIELDS FOREVER

Perth ● Dunkeld ● Blairgowrie ● Meigle ● Glamis
Brechin ● House of Dun ● Montrose ● Arbroath
Carnoustie ● Dundee ● Perth

The renowned 'Fair City' of Perth has a most attractive setting beside the River Tay. It was the county town of the former Perthshire and is very much the major town for the important farming communities in this region. In previous centuries, the medieval town built up traditional industries still celebrated in local street names such as Mill Street, Ropemakers Close and Glover Street. One fascinating reminder of traditional industry is the *Lower City Mills* which produces stoneground oatmeal and wheatflour from organically grown Scottish grain. There are also opportunities to discover something of today's occupations, the most notable being the *Caithness Glass Factory* and *Dewar's Whisky Bottling Plant*.

The history of the area and displays on the district's natural history feature in the fine *Museum and Art Gallery*. For visitors with an interest in gardens, Perth has the fine *Branklyn Gardens* and *Bell's Cherrybank Gardens*.

SPECIAL TO...

Much of the area, especially near Blairgowrie, is famous for its raspberries. Look for 'pick your own' signs where you can sample this delicious fruit.

ℹ️ 45 High Street, Perth; Caithness Glass Car Park, Almondbank, by the A9

*Leave by the **A912** and turn right at the **A9** (to Inverness). Turn right at the **A923** and follow this into Dunkeld (15 miles/24km).*

HM frigate Unicorn, *moored at the Victoria Dock in Dundee, is the oldest British warship still afloat. Today she provides an appropriate setting for a museum illustrating life in the Royal Navy during the days of sail*

Dunkeld, Tayside

1 The history of Dunkeld goes back to Pictish times but the town's importance in Scottish history is as Kenneth MacAlpin's ecclesiastical capital in the 9th century. This eventually led to the construction, in the early 14th century, of the **cathedral** which stands by the banks of the River Tay. Although much of it is roofless, the choir was restored and within it is the tomb of Alexander Stewart, the notorious 'Wolf of Badenoch'.

In the centre of Dunkeld stands a very ornate fountain and between this and the cathedral are the **Little Houses**, which were built in the late 17th century. Look out for the NTS's **The Ell Shop** on whose wall is an original ell measure, a little over a metre long, which was used for measuring cloth. Beside it is **The Duchess Anne**, formerly a school, which houses the cathedral **art exhibition** each summer.

ℹ️ The Cross

*Continue on the **A923** and follow it for 11 miles (18km) to Blairgowrie.*

Blairgowrie, Tayside

2 A bustling little town, Blairgowrie is well-situated as a touring centre, lying at the junction of five roads. The district's most remarkable feature is just 5 miles (8km) to the south on the A93: the magnificent **Meikleour Beech Hedge**. This was originally planted in 1746 and is now some 100 feet (30m) high and 2,000 feet (600m) long. It is trimmed by the local fire brigade!

ℹ️ Wellmeadow

*Leave by the **A926** then turn right at the **B954** to reach Meigle.*

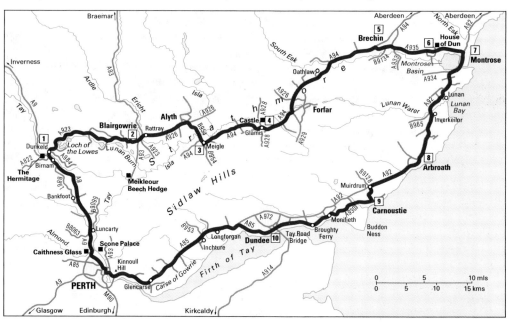

Meigle, Tayside

3 For such a small village, the local museum has a remarkable collection of carved stones. More than 30 significant stones have been found in the area and these portray ancient symbols such as Pictish beasts, a Persian god and a horseman. The dates vary, but are generally from the 8th to 10th centuries.

To add further interest to the local history, the village may have had connections with King Arthur – Queen Guinevere is said to be buried here.

*Leave by the **A94** to approach Glamis, then take a minor road on the left to reach the village and the castle.*

Glamis, Tayside

4 Glamis Castle, the childhood home of the Queen Mother, and birthplace of Princess Margaret, is an excellent example of a large medieval tower house that has, over the centuries, been transformed into a palace. The long straight driveway leads directly to its rather small entrance, an approach that seems to emphasize the symmetrical structure of the castle.

In comparison to the castle's grand style of living, the village of Glamis houses the Angus Folk Collection. This occupies a row of 18th-century cottages and contains furnished rooms from bygone days such as a kitchen, laundry, schoolhouse and a forge.

*Return to the **A94** and turn left. Follow the **A94**, then turn right at the **A935** to enter Brechin (17 miles/27km).*

The turreted and battlemented elegance of Glamis Castle, family home of the Bowes-Lyon Earls of Strathmore

Brechin, Tayside

5 The pleasant village of Brechin, with its many red sandstone buildings, lies in the heart of the rich agricultural area of Strathmore. Its most interesting feature, almost unique in Scotland, is the tall, slim round tower (11th-century) standing beside the 13th-century cathedral.

ⓘ St Ninian's Place

*Continue on the **A935** and follow it for 5 miles (8km) to the House of Dun. (The driveway is to the left.)*

House of Dun, Tayside

6 This 18th-century house was designed by William Adam, father of the Adam brothers who designed so many important buildings in Scotland. Recently restored by the NTS, it now reflects how it would have looked over 250 years ago with its public rooms featuring a wealth of exceptionally ornate baroque plasterwork.

*Continue on the **A935**, then turn right at the **A92** to enter Montrose (4 miles/6km).*

Montrose, Tayside

7 Montrose's wide main street lends an air of spaciousness to this seaside town. Its history, going back to the 10th century, owes much to the Montrose Basin which gave the town a uniquely strategic position on the

RECOMMENDED WALKS

Perth, Tayside **Kinnoull Hill,** which is about a mile (1.5km) from the centre of Perth, offers an outstanding view over the surrounding countryside.

1 *Dunkeld, Tayside* **The Hermitage** near Dunkeld is the site of a woodland walk in the care of the NTS. Two interesting follies and a waterfall make a stroll here a pleasant outing.

BACK TO NATURE

1 *Dunkeld, Tayside* The **Loch of the Lowes** lies to the east of Dunkeld and there are hides from which it is possible to see many birds, including ospreys and Slavonian grebes in the summer. In winter, look for greylag geese, pochards and goldeneye.

FOR CHILDREN

7 *Montrose, Tayside* The seaside resorts have good beaches but one 'remoter' stretch of sand can be found at the small village of **Lunan,** south of Montrose. The carpark at Lunan Bay's superb beach is reached by turning seawards just as the village is entered.

FOR HISTORY BUFFS

Perth, Tayside Perth became important when Scotland's first king, Kenneth MacAlpin, took the legendary **Stone of Destiny** to Scone Palace which lies just to the north of the town. Legend has it that this was the Biblical Jacob's pillow and it became the 'throne' upon which Scottish kings were crowned. In 1296, Edward I (the 'Hammer of the Scots') removed this symbol of Scottish nationhood to London's Westminster Abbey, but on Christmas Eve in 1950 the stone was taken by a small group of Scots. It 'disappeared' until 1952, when a stone was recovered at Arbroath Abbey – but whether or not it was the original stone or whether the real one is still in Scotland remains the subject of great debate.

SCENIC ROUTES

Hills are never very far away from much of this route and the views of the **Sidlaw Hills** and the foothills of the **Grampian Mountains** are good. On the drive to Dunkeld, it is interesting to note that the road is approaching a distinctive line of hills. These mark the geological boundary called the Highland Boundary Fault and indicate the 'real' start of the Scottish Highlands.

The stark remains of Arbroath Abbey, built and dedicated to St Thomas á Becket in the 13th century. The circular window in the south transept was lit in ancient times as a beacon to guide mariners

east coast. It has been an important port for a long time and its economy has recently enjoyed a boost with the emergence of the North Sea oil industry. Of more immediate interest to most visitors is the town's long beach which is backed by high sand dunes.

i The Library, High Street

> *Continue on the **A92** and follow it for 13 miles (21km) to Arbroath.*

Arbroath, Tayside

8 Arbroath is a busy seaside town whose beaches attract many visitors each summer. It also has an active fishing industry and this is the home of the delicious 'Arbroath smokie', a line-caught haddock that is smoke-cured using oak chips.

The town's place in Scots history was assured by the Declaration of Arbroath, a document drawn up in 1320 to state the independence of Scotland after the Battle of Bannockburn in 1314. The declaration was drawn up in the **abbey**, originally a priory founded in the 12th century.

i Market Place

> *Continue on the **A92**, then turn left at the **A930** to enter Carnoustie.*

Carnoustie, Tayside

9 Carnoustie's fame as a resort is based on its extensive **beach** and the **golf courses** which lie on the sandy links. The championship courses have played host to the Open a number of times.

i The Library, High Street

> *Continue on the **A930** for 11 miles (18km) to Dundee.*

Dundee, Tayside

10 The old saying that the industrial town of Dundee is famous for its jute, jam and journalism is less correct these days as the town's prosperity is now based on a much broader spectrum of industries.

Its coastal site has meant that the sea has always been of importance and many wooden ships for the whaling industry were built here. These ships had to withstand cruel polar conditions and this expertise was used in 1901 to build Captain Scott's ship *Discovery*, which is today berthed only a short distance from the city centre. Close to it is the frigate *Unicorn*, built in 1825.

The city's history is told in the **McManus Galleries**, which also hold the local art collection; the **Barrack Street Museum** houses a natural history collection including the skeleton of a whale. The city's connections with the whaling industry are displayed in the 15th-century **Broughty Castle Museum** which occupies a prominent position guarding the entrance to the Firth of Tay.

i 4 City Square

> *Leave by the **A85** and follow it for 22 miles (35km) back to Perth.*

Perth – Dunkeld **15 (24)**
Dunkeld – Blairgowrie **11 (18)**
Blairgowrie – Meigle **8 (13)**
Meigle – Glamis **7 (11)**
Glamis – Brechin **17 (27)**
Brechin – House of Dun **5 (8)**
House of Dun – Montrose **4 (6)**
Montrose – Arbroath **13 (21)**
Arbroath – Carnoustie **7 (11)**
Carnoustie – Dundee **11 (18)**
Dundee – Perth **22 (35)**

THE KINGDOM OF FIFE

A royal plaque of 1610 built into a wall of a Falkland cottage. Falkland Palace was a favourite seat of the Scottish Court from the reign of King James V

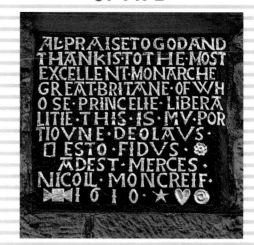

ⓘ 78 South Street

*Leave by the **A917** and follow it for 10 miles (16km) to Crail.*

Crail, Fife

1 Crail's small harbour is a delightful and much photographed place set at the bottom of a steep lane; crab and lobster fishing is carried out from here. Early prosperity stemmed from trading and fishing, and the history of the community is told in the small **museum** in Marketgate.

ⓘ Crail Museum and Heritage Centre

*Continue on the **A917** and follow it for 4 miles (6km) to Anstruther.*

Anstruther, Fife

2 The Scottish Fisheries Museum, which is situated on the seafront, tells the story of fishing and the fisherfolk from this part of the country. In the harbour are moored two of the museum's great attractions, the *North Carr Lightship* (which was stationed off Fife Ness until 1976) and the fishing boat *The Reaper*. One of the houses in the main street is completely decorated with seashells.

ⓘ East Neuk Information Centre, Scottish Fisheries Museum

*Continue on the **A917** for 1 mile (2km) to Pittenweem.*

Crow-stepped and red-tiled houses cluster round Crail harbour, once the haunt of smugglers. The town is East Neuk's oldest Royal Burgh

St Andrews ● Crail ● Anstruther ● Pittenweem
St Monans ● Elie ● Falkland ● Scotlandwell ● Kinross
Abernethy ● Cupar ● St Andrews

St Andrews is famous as the golfing capital of the world and a round on the fine courses of the *Royal and Ancient Golf Club* has become something of a pilgrimage for huge numbers of golfers from around the globe. Written records for the *Old Course*, the oldest in the world, date back to the 15th century. The *British Golf Museum* is situated close to the clubhouse.

The town's early importance came from the establishment of the cathedral in 1160. Most of it is now in ruins but 12th-century *St Rule's Tower* is still in good condition and its parapet gives fine views of the town. The 12th-century *castle* is near the cathedral and stands on a rocky promontory overlooking the sea.

The Reformation led to the decline of the cathedral, and ultimately the town, until the 18th century when the growing influence of the ancient university became an important factor in the town's renaissance. The *university* (founded in 1410, and Britain's third oldest, after Oxford and Cambridge) occupies many fine buildings in the town as well as a modern campus on the outskirts.

SCENIC ROUTES

The journey through the fishing villages of **East Neuk** is very pleasant. Not only are the 'vernacular' houses attractive, there are also views of the coastline, the Isle of May and the opposite shore of the Firth of Forth, with Edinburgh an obvious landmark.

Near Loch Leven there are pleasing views of the Lomond Hills which rise steeply from the surrounding rich farmland.

The gate to St Fillan's Cave, Pittenweem. It is said that a light shone from his arm one day when he was writing in dim light

premises than in the neighbouring villages, the result of the town being 'dry' between 1900 and 1947.

To the southwest are the ruins of 17th-century **Newark Castle**.

Continue on the A917 for 3 miles (5km) to Elie.

Elie, Fife

5 This appealing resort offers fine sandy beaches and bathing, golf courses and shelter to the yachts that lie in the harbour. The sea has not always been kind to Elie and the houses along the bay have high walls to protect them. There are many fine 17th-century houses in South Street.

Continue on the A917 to Upper Largo, then join the A915 to Windygates. Join the A911 and head towards Glenrothes. Turn right at a roundabout at the junction with the A92 and head northwards. Turn left when the A912 is met and follow this to Falkland (21 miles/34km).

Falkland, Fife

6 The village of Falkland is dominated by the very grand **palace**, which was originally erected by the Stuarts as a royal hunting seat. It dates from the 16th century on a site that has been fortified from the 13th century. The buildings on the southern side of the main courtyard are in a fine state of preservation and have some excellent furnishings; the painted wooden ceilings are particularly good. Within the grounds is a **Royal Tennis Court**, built in 1539 for James V, before rackets were invented. The game was originally played with the hand, which was protected by a leather glove.

The village itself has numerous fascinating small houses, many of them dating back to the 17th and 18th centuries. The **museum** in the main street has displays that explain the local history.

Continue on the A912 and turn left at the A91 and left again at the B919. Turn left at the A911 and follow it to Scotlandwell.

SPECIAL TO...

One common feature of the smaller houses in many of the Fife villages are the red pantiles, roofing tiles with a double curve. Although they look like attractive and costly embellishments, they were originally used as they were cheaper than (and inferior to) slates. Since they have only small overlaps they often need a lot of mortar between them to keep the roof watertight. Many of the harbourside houses have pantiled roofs.

RECOMMENDED WALKS

The coastal path from St Monans to Elie offers an interesting route past St Monans' church, the ruins of two castles (Newark and Ardross) and ends at Elie Ness with its fine view of the village.

Inland, the walk to the top of East Lomond above Falkland gives good views over the village and the surrounding countryside.

Pittenweem, Fife

3 The busiest fishing port along this coast, there is always lots to see in Pittenweem when the boats are coming in with their catches. Herring used to be the major catch here but now the fishermen concentrate on white fish.

The religious buildings date back many centuries: the parish church's **tower** was built in the 16th century and there are remains of a 12th-century **priory** where witches were 'done to death'.

Nearby **St Fillan's Cave** is said to be the 7th-century sanctuary of St Fillan. It gave Pittenweem its name (Pittenweem is Pictish for The Place of the Cave).

Continue on the A917 for 2 miles (3km) to St Monans.

St Monans, Fife

4 St Monans (or St Monance) is a pleasant fishing town, with houses clustered around the local harbour. Boat building and repairing are still local trades.

One rather unusual feature of the town is that it has fewer licensed

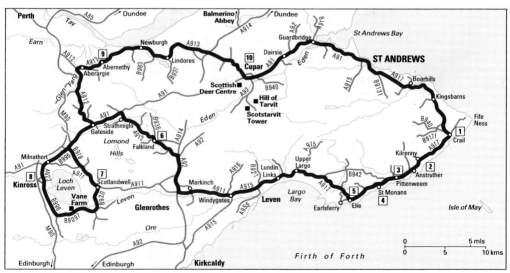

Scotlandwell, Tayside

7 The village is named after the well, a sort of early spa, to which pilgrims travelled during medieval times. Roman soldiers are said to have drunk from it in AD84. However, the present stone cistern dates back only to the 19th century.

Leave by the B920 and turn right at the B9097. Take another right turn when the B996 is met and follow it to Kinross.

Kinross, Tayside

8 Kinross, the county town of the former Kinross-shire, stands by the shores of **Loch Leven**. Of the loch's two largest islands, **St Serf's Island** has the remains of a priory which was founded around the 9th century.

Castle Island is rather nearer the town and can be reached by a local ferry. On it stands **Loch Leven Castle**, best known as the prison in which Mary, Queen of Scots was kept from 1567 to 1568. The castle originates from the 14th century and the building and its garden used to occupy the whole of the island until in the early 19th century the loch's level was lowered, increasing the size of the island. The castle, a five-storey keep, was occupied for about 250 years but was roofless by the end of the 17th century. Although it was inhabited for such a long time, it was little altered and stands as a good example of how a 14th-century fortification of this type looked.

i Kinross Service Area, M90

Continue on the B996 and join the A922. After Milnathort, follow the B996 then the A91. Turn left at the A912 and right at the A913 to Abernethy, 13 miles (21km).

Abernethy, Tayside

9 One of the main features of this quiet little village is the 11th-century **round tower**, very similar to Brechin's. Abernethy may have been an important centre in Pictish times and several symbol stones have been found in the vicinity; one of them is set against the wall of the tower.

Continue on the A913 and follow it for 13 miles (21km) to Cupar.

Cupar, Fife

10 It is rather surprising that this little town, and not St Andrews, was the county town of Fife, but this was due to its central position and because it was the seat of the Thanes (ancient chieftains) of Fife.

Cupar must surely have a place in the history of drama as it was here in 1535 that the first public performance of the satire *Ane satire of the Thrie Estaits* took place. This scorned the church, the nobility and the burgesses of the towns, the three 'estates' that made up the country's ruling bodies. The play has certainly stood the test of time and it is still performed on the Scottish stage.

To the south of Cupar stands the **Hill of Tarvit**, a mansion house under the ownership of the NTS. The present building was built at the beginning of the 20th century to house a fine collection of antique furniture, much of it French. To the west of it is **Scotstarvit Tower**, a well-preserved five-storey towerhouse built in the 17th century.

i Fluthers Car Park

Leave by the A91 and follow it for 10 miles (16km) back to St Andrews.

St Andrews – Crail **10 (16)**
Crail – Anstruther **4 (6)**
Anstruther – Pittenweem **1 (2)**
Pittenweem – St Monans **2 (3)**
St Monans – Elie **3 (5)**
Elie – Falkland **21 (34)**
Falkland – Scotlandwell **12 (19)**
Scotlandwell – Kinross **8 (13)**
Kinross – Abernethy **13 (21)**
Abernethy – Cupar **13 (21)**
Cupar – St Andrews **10 (16)**

An advantageous view of the layout of St Andrew's Cathedral seen from the tower of closeby St Regulus' (Rule's) Church

BACK TO NATURE

8 *Kinross, Tayside* **Vane Farm**, situated at the southern end of Loch Leven, is a nature reserve run by the RSPB. This is one of Europe's most important wildfowl sites and different types of geese, such as pink-footed, greylag, barnacle, brent, Canada, white-fronted and the occasional snow, can be seen during the winter. Many ducks nest here during the summer, especially on St Serf's Island, and these can be seen from the hides.

FOR HISTORY BUFFS

10 *Cupar, Fife* Ruined **Balmerino Abbey**, which lies by the shores of the Firth of Tay, northeast of Cupar, was a Cistercian abbey founded in the 13th century. The beautiful chapter house dates from the 15th century. A Spanish chestnut tree in the grounds is said to have been planted by the monks.

FOR CHILDREN

Fife has many glorious beaches to keep children busy for hours on end; St Andrews, Elie and Largo Bay have some of the most extensive.

10 *Cupar, Fife* Although Fife has no high hills to give shelter to deer, the **Scottish Deer Centre** has been established just to the west of Cupar and various species of deer can be seen. Children can also help with bottle feeding the fawns and the deer can be stroked and touched.

THE NORTHEAST

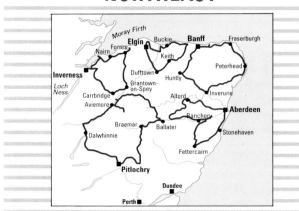

The village of Fochabers viewed across the pond by the old railway station. The slender, classical spire of Bellie Kirk pierces the sky to the left. It was the last major work of the architect John Baxter

The Cairngorm mountains, Britain's highest land mass, dominate the northeast of Scotland in many ways. The great glaciers that flowed down from these granite hills during the Ice Age cut their way through the rock, leaving behind a series of river valleys that radiate from the mountains and flow down to the sea.

In days gone by, it was easier to travel by sea than land and this encouraged coastal settlements to prosper wherever there was a sheltered harbour and the opportunity to trade with other ports, notably those in countries across the North Sea. Today, fishing is of great importance and this coastline boasts some of Britain's most important fishing harbours. But while the fishing industry is long established, it is the new North Sea oil developments that have transformed the Aberdeen area and made that city Scotland's 'oil capital'.

The northeast lies in the hills' rain shadow, making this region much drier than the west coast and helping to produce some of Scotland's most profitable farming land. Agriculture continues to be an important industry and much of the region's population lives in scattered towns and villages set among good agricultural land.

The often turbulent times of the Middle Ages saw the establishment of a class of rich farmers, warriors and traders who built keeps, castles and fortified houses. In time, many of these were destroyed while others were extended and embellished and some later transformed into great country houses. Today, we are left with a rich legacy of castles, both large and small, that reflect the changing fortunes of family, clan and nation. Many enchanted visitors have compared Deeside with the splendour of the Loire Valley.

The wide variety of landscapes is reflected in the wildlife found in the region. The hills and the high forests are home to deer and birds of prey while the coast, with its sandstone cliffs providing ledges for nesting birds, has countless millions of seabirds.

Walkers, birdwatchers, fishing enthusiasts, families seeking tranquil beaches and visitors simply touring around will all find lots to do in this pleasant and fascinating corner of Scotland. To many foreign visitors, Scotland is famous as the home of whisky, and in the northeast a number of internationally famous distilleries are linked together by the 'Whisky Trail', which allows people to learn the secrets of the whisky-making process and, inevitably, to enjoy a 'wee dram' at the end of a distillery tour.

Tour 14

Inverness' strategic position at the meeting point of so many land and sea routes has meant that the town and its surrounding district have seen the comings and goings of many different peoples. Picts, Vikings and warring Scots clans have all left their mark, but the most significant historical event, the battle of Culloden in 1746, has left its mark all over Scotland; in order to understand the history of the Highlands, the battlefield should be visited. This tour encompasses a wide variety of scenery, from the glorious sandy beaches of the Moray Firth to the pine forests that lie below the Cairngorms.

Tour 15

The seaside towns and villages of Moray have much to offer the visitor: picturesque harbours, sandy beaches and a wealth of traditional buildings that give the district its own particular charm. Inland, the districts by the peaty waters of the River Spey are home to many of Scotland's most celebrated whisky distilleries.

Tour 16

The coastal part of this route visits a variety of harbours, from the small picture-postcard ones like charming Crovie to the big, bustling Peterhead. Each has its own fascination and each reflects the ways in which the sea has been so important to the people of this area. Behind this, the rich countryside, with its landscape of rolling hills, has prosperous farming towns and villages. The long history of settlement in this part of the country is marked by the existence of prehistoric stone circles.

Above: Shiny, gleaming coppers at the Fettercairn Distillery
Right: The subdued ruins of one of Scotland's largest castles, Urquhart Castle on Strone Point, above Loch Ness. The castle was blown up in 1692 to prevent Jacobite occupation

Tour 17

The fact that this tour is the longest one in the region reflects the sheer scale of the Cairngorms. Motorists have to drive round the margins of the hills, but this does allow the visitor many different opportunities to explore the small glens that cut into the sides of these great mountains. There is much variety on the route; the traditional highland resort of Pitlochry, the more modern and brasher Aviemore and the small villages that lie to the east. Walkers will find much to keep them busy on this tour as will followers of other outdoor pursuits, from pony trekking to hang gliding.

Tour 18

The visitor to this part of the country might be forgiven for getting the impression there's a castle round every corner! But the district has more to offer than fine old buildings; there are peaceful villages, a rugged coast-line and rich agricultural countryside to explore.

1/2 days – 106 miles (169km)

LAND OF MACBETH

Inverness ● Fort George ● Cawdor Castle ● Nairn
Brodie Castle ● Forres ● Findhorn ● Grantown-on-Spey
Carrbridge ● Culloden ● Inverness

With all the amenities of an important town, Inverness has highland scenery on its very doorstep. Its 19th-century *castle* stands above the River Ness and upstream are the delightful Ness Islands, linked by bridges to allow access from one bank to the other. A short walk from the islands leads to the *Caledonian Canal*. Cruises are available here and the walk along the canal's towpath from the locks at Bucht Park to the terminus in the Beauly Firth is pleasant.

High Street is the most important thoroughfare in Inverness and here is the *Town House*, erected in the late 19th century. *Abertarff House* in Church Street is the town's oldest house, having been built in about 1592. *Queen Mary's House* in Bridge Street was visited by the queen in 1562. The history of the town is told in the *Inverness Art Gallery and Museum*, situated near the castle.

A commemorative plaque on the 1881 memorial cairn dedicated to the Highlanders who gave their lives at the Battle of Culloden. Defeat ended the Jacobite cause, and the days of the 'wild Scots' were over

ℹ 23 Church Street

*Leave on the **A96**. Turn left at the **B9039** to reach Ardersier, then take the **B9006** to Fort George, 12 miles (19km).*

Fort George, Highland

1 This outstanding piece of military architecture, which is still used by the army, was originally built between 1748 and 1769, after the battle of Culloden. It was guarded by 2,000 men and it has a series of walls, ramparts and ditches cleverly designed so that an attacking army would come under fire from several positions within the safety of the fort. It controls the seaward approach to Inverness as it is sited on a promontory that juts into the Moray Firth; this is rather fortunate for visitors as it allows good views across the firth to the Black Isle.

The fort is impressively huge, indeed the whole of Edinburgh Castle could fit into the parade ground! Since the fort has never seen military action, very few alterations have been made to its layout and a number of original buildings have been opened to visitors.

The B9006, which leads to the fort, was one of the military roads built by Caulfield in the 18th century when the government was trying to 'tame' this area. It follows the much older Via Regis (King's Road) which came from Aberdeen and crossed the Moray Firth to Chanonry Point at Fortrose.

*Return to Ardersier, then follow the **B9006** and the **B9090** to Cawdor Castle, 8 miles (13km).*

FOR HISTORY BUFFS

3 *Nairn, Highland* **Ardclach Bell Tower**, southeast of Nairn, off the **A939**, was built in 1655 when the local laird, a Covenanter, was continually being harassed by Royalists. The tower served both as a prison and a watchtower and its bell was used to summon people to the local church.

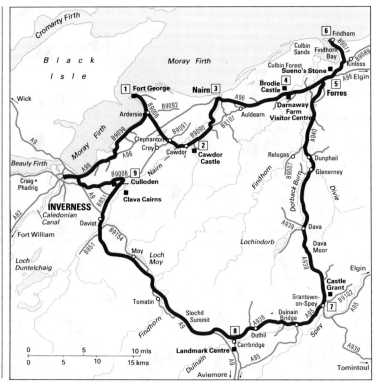

Cawdor Castle, Highland

2 The castle is dominated by the great 14th-century tower. Later additions had far less of a defensive role to play since they were built in less turbulent times. Still, the castle has many of the features that might be expected of a fortified house such as a drawbridge, a moat and a prison that was reached only by a trap door. The proprietors of Cawdor were called the Thanes of Cawdor, a title given by Shakespeare to Macbeth, but there is still much speculation about the real nature of this warrior king.

To the west stands 15th-century **Kilravock Castle**, a massive tower with walls some 7 feet (2m) thick. The tower has survived through the centuries, despite the laird backing the losing side at Culloden, and the victor, Cumberland, paying it a visit after the battle. Few castles in a similar position survived a visit by the 'Butcher'.

*Continue on the **B9090** and follow it for 5 miles (8km) into Nairn.*

Nairn, Highland

3 This popular holiday resort, situated where the River Nairn meets the Moray Firth, has a fine beach, good golf course and activities for family holidays. Charlie Chaplin's favourite holiday resort for many years, it is a prosperous town, with large villas and hotels behind the main centre. Nearer the shore, the former fishermen's houses are tightly packed together in Fishertown where there is a small museum.

To the east, the village of **Auldearn** was the site of a major battle in 1645

Pebbles glow golden in the dying light of day, heaped high by winter storms. This is Spey Bay, the terminal stage in the journey of Scotland's second longest river

when the Royalist army defeated a force of Covenanters. The battleground can be seen from the top of a 12th-century motte, upon which now sits a 17th-century **doocot** (dovecot) which has 546 nest holes for pigeons.

i 62 King Street

*Leave by the **A96** and turn left at the entrance to Brodie Castle, 7 miles (11km).*

Brodie Castle, Grampian

4 Originally, the castle had a Z-plan design, based on a rectangular block with square projecting towers at two opposite corners. This structure, dated 1567, was later added to and has had many alterations over the centuries. Inside the castle is a good collection of 17th-, 18th- and 19th-century paintings and French furniture.

At the eastern entrance to the castle stands the Pictish **Rodney's Stone**, decorated with a Pictish beast and fish monsters.

*Regain the **A96** and continue on it for 4 miles (6km) to Forres.*

Forres, Grampian

5 The street pattern in Forres gives clues to the town's antiquity, with a main street wide enough to accommodate a market place and narrow 'wynds' linking the medieval streets. High Street is dominated by the **Town House** of 1838, built on the

FOR CHILDREN

2 *Cawdor Castle, Highland* At the **Nairn Farm Sheep Dairy**, near Cawdor Castle, you can watch sheep being milked and see how their milk is used to make cheese.

5 *Forres, Highland* To the west of Forres, the **Darnaway Farm Visitor Centre** gives people the opportunity to see a working dairy farm. There is also an exhibition on forestry.

6 *Findhorn, Highland* As well as being endowed with long sandy beaches which will keep children busy for hours on end, Findhorn is a centre for watersports, with sailing, rowing, windsurfing and water skiing available.

The delightfully precarious single arch of Carrbridge packhorse bridge over the River Dulnain. The structure was built by the Earl of Seafield for the use of funeral parties travelling to Duthil

site of the old Tolbooth, and the market cross which was erected in 1844. The **Falconer Museum** in Tolbooth Street has displays of local history, natural history and geology.

The town's main antiquity lies just to the east of Forres, as the B9011 leaves the A96. This is **Sueno's Stone**, a huge cross-slab monument, over 20 feet (6m) high, carved out of a block of sandstone. It may date back to the 9th century and celebrate a victory by the men of Moray over Vikings based in Orkney.

[i] Falconer Museum, Tolbooth Street

Continue on the A96 then turn left at the B9011 and follow this to Findhorn.

Findhorn, Grampian

6 This is the third village on this site to bear the name of Findhorn. The first was destroyed by the sea and the second was inundated by shifting sand. The people rebuilt the village near the sea and it was once a prominent port, but its harbour is now given over to pleasure craft. The beaches here are extensive, with huge

stretches of sand and dunes along the coast on either side of the River Findhorn's estuary.

Return along the B9011 and A96 to Forres. Head south on the A940 and join the A939 to reach Grantown-on-Spey, 27 miles (43km).

Grantown-on-Spey, Highland

7 This prosperous village, with its sturdy granite buildings along the main street, is a good touring centre for the district. It began as a planned village and from the start gained a reputation as a place to which Victorian doctors would send patients who were in need of a change of air. Today it is noted for its salmon fishing, and walkers, anglers and families frequent the village during the summer, while in winter it offers accommodation to many skiers.

Standing just to the north of the village, **Castle Grant** was started in the 15th century but greatly altered in later centuries. Robert Burns visited here during his Highland travels and so did Queen Victoria – though she was not impressed, describing it as a 'very plain looking house, like a factory'.

[i] High Street

Leave on the A95 towards Aviemore, and at Dulnain Bridge turn on to the A938 to Carrbridge.

Carrbridge, Highland

8 The old bridge at Carrbridge was built in 1717 after two men drowned at the fording place. The bridge has since lost many of its stones and is precariously balanced over the river making it one of the most photogenic bridges in the country.

The village is a popular touring centre, all the more so because of the nearby **Landmark Centre**, which tells the story of how people have lived in the Highlands. It is set within a pine forest and has many walks, including a tree-top trail 20 feet (6m) above the ground.

ⓘ Main Street

*Continue on the **A938** and join the **A9**, heading towards Inverness. Leave this road after Daviot, when the **B851** is met. Turn left at the **B9006** and follow it to the NTS (National Trust for Scotland) Visitor Centre at Culloden Moor, a total of 23 miles (37km).*

Culloden, Highland

9 Many bloody battles have been fought on Scottish soil, but of all the country's battlefields, Culloden is the saddest. Here, in 1746, the last great battle fought on British soil ended forever the Jacobite hopes of regaining the British crown. It was not a battle of Scots against English, nor was it a battle between different parts of Scotland, but it was the final battle of a long civil war. In its bloody aftermath, the face of the Highlands was changed forever. After the government's victory, the might of the British army was used to subjugate Scotland and to destroy many aspects of the Highlanders' way of life.

The battlefield has been laid out to show how the Government troops, led by the Duke of Cumberland, faced the army of Charles Edward Stuart (the 'Bonnie Prince Charlie' of song and legend). Displays in the visitor centre

describe the course of that dreadful battle, and the equally violent events that followed. Various small memorials on the battlefield indicate where particular clans were buried where they fell, but the principal monument is the **Memorial Cairn**, erected in 1881. The battle was fought on open moorland and **Old Leanach Cottage**, which was standing at the time of the battle, still remains. Its reconstructed interior illustrates how Scots people lived at the time of the battle in the mid-18th century.

A little to the east of Culloden, a minor road passes **Clava Cairns**, some of the most important cairns in the country. The three cairns may have been erected in the Late Stone Age or Early Bronze Age. The two outer ones are called 'passage graves' as a small passageway led through the cairn to a central chamber where bodies or cremated remains were deposited. These cairns have been topped with a massive flat slab and their perimeters were (and still are) marked by a ring of standing stones. Many of these perimeter stones have 'cup marks', small round indentations of unknown origin.

ⓘ Daviot Wood, on the **A9**

*Return along the **B9006** to the **A9**. Join the **A9** and return to Inverness, 5 miles (8km).*

Inverness – Fort George **12 (19)**
Fort George – Cawdor Castle **8 (13)**
Cawdor Castle – Nairn **5 (8)**
Nairn – Brodie Castle **7 (11)**
Brodie Castle – Forres **4 (6)**
Forres – Findhorn **5 (8)**
Findhorn – Grantown-on-Spey **27 (43)**
Grantown-on-Spey – Carrbridge **10 (16)**
Carrbridge – Culloden **23 (37)**
Culloden – Inverness **5 (8)**

Inverness Castle fronted by Flora Macdonald's memorial. The statue shows the Jacobite heroine looking southwest towards Bonnie Prince Charlie's hiding place

1/2 days – 89 miles (144km)

THE WHISKY TRAIL

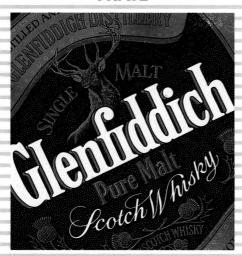

Elgin ● Lossiemouth ● Fochabers ● Spey Bay
Buckie ● Cullen ● Portsoy ● Keith ● Dufftown
Rothes ● Elgin

The busy town of Elgin has many fine buildings, the principal one being the *cathedral*. This was founded in 1224 but in 1390 Alexander Stewart, the 'Wolf of Badenoch', burned both the cathedral and town in revenge for his excommunication by the local bishop. However, restoration work still continues. Elgin's royal *castle* stood on Lady Hill from the 12th to the 15th centuries; there are few traces remaining but the hill is made very conspicuous by the tall column erected in honour of the last Duke of Gordon.

Many of the town's medieval features are preserved. The High Street still runs between the cathedral and the castle and the basic street layout is intact. There is still the cobbled market place and narrow wynds (alleyways) that link the streets. *Elgin Museum* has good displays of local material with special features on geology, archaeology and natural history, and the *Moray Motor Museum* in Bridge Street, has vintage cars and examples of classic two- and four-wheel vehicles.

FOR CHILDREN

1 *Lossiemouth, Grampian* The coast has many good beaches, which makes this area popular with families. Lossiemouth has two beaches; the east one is suitable for surfing while the west one offers safe bathing.
Buckie, Elgin and Keith have swimming pools, and pony trekking is available at **Drybridge** (near Buckie) and **Garmouth** (near Fochabers). Cullen has a long sandy beach in front of the golf course.

Whisky Galore! Scotland's most famous export represented here by the distinctive label of the Glenfiddich Distillery, Dufftown

🛈 17 High Street

*Leave Elgin on the **A941** and follow it north for 6 miles (10km) to Lossiemouth.*

Lossiemouth, Grampian

1 This was developed as a port for landlocked Elgin after its original port of Spynie was cut off from the sea by shifting sand. It later became important during the 19th-century herring boom but today the catches are mainly shellfish and white fish.

Lossiemouth is now a popular seaside resort, with extensive sandy beaches and a championship golf course. The **Lossiemouth Fishery and Community Museum** features many aspects of local life and also has a display dedicated to Ramsay MacDonald, the first Labour Prime Minister, who was born locally.

Just inland stand the ruins of the 15th-century **Palace of Spynie**, once the seat of the Bishops of Moray.

Duffus Castle is to the southwest of Lossiemouth in an area of flat, fertile farmland, lying only a few feet above sea level. This was a swamp when the original motte-and-bailey castle was built. A massive tower was added around 1300. Unfortunately the gravel foundations could not support the extra weight and part of the building's walls gave way and slid downhill.

*Return along the **A941** and turn left at the **B9103**. Turn left at the **A96** and continue to Fochabers.*

The surviving twin towers of Elgin Cathedral supply a hint to the magnificence that must have once existed

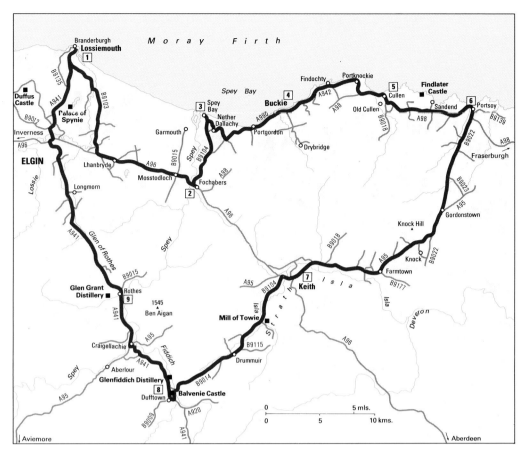

Fochabers, Grampian

2 Fochabers was originally situated within the grounds of Gordon Castle but was demolished at the end of the 18th century to make way for an extension to the castle. When it was being re-established in its present position, the streets were laid out in a grid pattern, and there still remains a wealth of well-built Georgian houses, especially along its main street.

The village's position beside the River Spey led to its growing importance as a river-crossing point, though no bridge crossed the river here until 1804 when the ferry was superseded by **Fochabers Old Bridge**. The river's east bank offers good walks and paths leading southward from the village to the very unusual 'earth pillars' which were formed by erosion of the huge quantities of sand and pebble deposits that were laid down here by the Spey.

The factory of Baxters of Speyside is where the well-known tinned soups and other foodstuffs are made and tours round the premises are available. The original **Baxter's grocery shop**, where the family's soups were first sold in Spey Street, has been reconstructed in the visitor centre and there is also a Victorian kitchen, showing how the family meals were prepared in the 19th century.

The Fochabers **Folk Museum** in High Street has displays outlining the local history, as well as a costume collection and a display of horse-drawn vehicles.

*Return along the **A96**, then turn right at the **B9104** to Spey Bay, 5 miles (8km).*

Spey Bay, Grampian

3 The River Spey is Scotland's second longest river with a length of 98 miles (158km) and it drains a large area of high ground, including part of the Cairngorms. Huge quantities of ice and water flowed down the river during the Ice Age, accounting for its great width and the massive deposits of sand and gravel brought down at various stages of its history. At Spey Bay, where the river meets the sea, the river dumps the material it has brought downstream and the huge volume of peaty water stains the sea for quite a distance offshore.

Longshore drift has encouraged a huge shingle spit to form at the river's mouth and salmon fishers have traditionally netted fish from this point. The **Tugnet Ice-House**, built in 1830 to store the ice that was used for packing salmon, stands near by. This is Scotland's largest ice-house and it has been restored to take on its new role as a museum that tells the story of the salmon fishery.

The bay is the northern terminus for the **Speyside Way**, the long-distance footpath that follows the river for part of its lower course.

*Return along the **B9104** and turn left at an unclassified road to Portgordon. Follow the roads to Portgordon, then join the **A990** and follow it to Buckie.*

Buckie, Grampian

4 Buckie stretches for about 3 miles (5km) along the coast and has developed through the amalgamation of smaller fishing communities. Its main harbour is very busy and the area behind it still has many traditional fishermen's houses dating back to the

RECOMMENDED WALKS

The **Speyside Way** offers an opportunity to discover much about the district and leaflets describing the various stages of the Way are available in the tourist information centres.

There are also many good coastal walks offering fine views of the coastline. One interesting walk starts at **Sandend** (which is between Portsoy and Cullen) and follows the clifftop path to **Findlater Castle**; a return route past an old 'doocot' (dovecot) allows a circular walk to be made.

BACK TO NATURE

3 *Spey Bay, Grampian* The sandy coastline is home to many birds who search for food when the tide is out. Spey Bay can be particularly good for birdwatchers with terns, waders, oystercatchers and curlews to be sighted; look out for seals a little offshore.

FOR HISTORY BUFFS

Elgin, Grampian To the northwest of Elgin stands the ruin of **Duffus Castle**, on a site that has been fortified from at least the mid-12th century. Originally it was a motte-and-bailey castle and the deep defensive ditch of that time is still there. The stone castle now on the motte may date back to the 14th century.

SPECIAL TO ...

The proximity of so many distilleries makes sampling the local whiskies a popular pastime for many visitors. The richness of the local fishing grounds means that many delicious fresh seafood dishes should be available locally, and in Cullen why not try the local delicacy, **Cullen Skink**, a broth based on smoked haddock?

19th century. The town's rich fishing tradition features strongly in the displays in the **Buckie Maritime Museum**.

The neighbouring village of **Portgordon** was once a centre for salmon fishing and near the harbour stands a restored **ice-house** that was built in 1834.

i Cluny Square

*Leave by the **A942** via Findochty and Portknockie. Turn left at the **A98** and follow this to Cullen, 8 miles (13km).*

Cullen, Grampian

5 The most obvious feature of this pleasant seaside village is the tall and graceful railway viaduct that slices Cullen in two. Trains no longer run on the line but its route is now part of a coastal path.

Below the arches, the seaward part of the village has a little harbour with fishermen's houses and a fine stretch of beach. The golf course is jammed in between the shore and the former sea cliffs and on the course's seaward side stand the 'Three Kings', three tall sea stacks that have managed to withstand the onslaught of the pounding seas. The Square has many interesting buildings round it, notably the old **Town Hall**. The very ornate **mercat (market) cross** was not originally in the Square, but came from Old Cullen which shared the same fate as the original Fochabers, and was demolished because the local laird felt the village was too close to his house. **Cullen Auld Kirk**, which is still in Old Cullen, dates from the 16th century and contains some fine stone carvings.

At the western end of Cullen Bay is the curious **Bow Fiddle Rock**, an island with a natural arch that is probably best seen from the small village of **Portknockie**, which can be reached via a clifftop path.

To the east of the village stand the ruins of the 15th-century **Findlater Castle**. This was owned by the Ogilvies but abandoned around 1600 in preference to the more comfortable Cullen House.

Empty, wooden whisky barrels awaiting reclamation at the Strathisla Distillery, Keith. The oak casks serve as a maturing stage in the production process

i 20 Seafield Street

*Continue on the **A98** for 6 miles (10km) to Portsoy.*

Portsoy, Grampian

6 Portsoy's sheltered harbour was once considered to be one of the safest in this part of Scotland, an attribute that did much to hasten the port's growth.

The village's great claim to fame, however, was its fine vein of pink and green serpentine, in great demand for its beauty. Some of it was used in the Palace of Versailles. This tradition still lives on and the harbourside **Portsoy Marble Workshop** has good examples of rock-based ornaments on sale.

*Leave by the **A98** and turn right at the **B9022**. Join the **A95** and follow it to Keith, a distance of 17 miles (27km).*

Keith, Grampian

7 Keith's role as an important centre for the rich neighbouring farmland reaches its high point each year at the **Agricultural Show**. Traditional farming ways have been preserved in part at **Mill of Towie** (to the south of Keith) where oatmeal is produced in a restored 19th-century mill.

The town lies in the broad valley of Strath Isla, hence the name of the local **Strathisla Distillery**. This is on the celebrated 'Whisky Trail', a route connecting a number of distilleries that welcome visitors to their premises. Strathisla is the Highlands' oldest working distillery: production started in 1786, though illicit brewing and distilling may have taken place on the site as far back as the 13th century.

i Church Road

*Leave on the **A96** (to Inverness), then turn left at the **B9014** which leads into Dufftown, 11 miles (18km).*

Dufftown, Grampian

8 The centre of the village is dominated by the battlemented **Clock Tower** that was built in 1839. The tower has had a varied life, having first been the local jail, then the burgh (borough) chambers and now a small museum. The clock on the tower came from Banff and played a major part in the hanging of the unlucky James MacPherson. This poor fellow was a popular figure who had been

robbing the rich and giving the pro-
ceeds to the poor, and a petition was
raised to obtain a pardon for him. This
was successful, but while the pardon
was on its way, the local sheriff put
the town's clock forward by an hour,
making sure that the prisoner was
duly dispatched before the reprieve
arrived!

Dufftown is the home of the
Glenfiddich Distillery, which is on the
Whisky Trail. Production started here
in 1887 and, very unusually, the
product is bottled on the premises.

The substantial ruins of Balvenie
Castle lie close to the village. This was
a massive building surrounding a
central courtyard with a curtain wall
7 feet (2m) thick.

[i] The Square

*Leave by the **A941** and follow it
for 7 miles (11km) to Rothes.*

*Solid, sturdy buildings of
indigenous rock monitor the
movements of shipping in Portsoy
harbour. Immovable walls provide
reassuringly obstinate protection
from the storms of the Moray Firth*

Rothes, Grampian

9 On the journey from Dufftown to
Rothes the A941 crosses the River
Spey near the village of Craigellachie.
Just upstream from this crossing
stands a very graceful iron bridge,
built by Thomas Telford between
1812 and 1815 to withstand huge
floods when the river was swollen
with spring meltwater. Its great test
came in 1829 when it survived a rise
in water level of 15½ feet (4.5m). This
is the country's oldest surviving iron
bridge.

Founded in 1766 as a crofting
township (a croft may be best described as a Scottish smallholding),
Rothes developed into an important
centre for distilling as no fewer than
five distilleries were working here at
one time. The Glen Grant Distillery,
which is on the Whisky Trail, was
started in 1840 by two brothers and
their whisky was one of the first to be
bottled as a 'single malt'.

*Continue on the **A941** for
10 miles (16km) to return to
Elgin.*

Elgin – Lossiemouth **6 (10)**
Lossiemouth – Fochabers **13 (21)**
Fochabers – Spey Bay **5 (8)**
Spey Bay – Buckie **6 (10)**
Buckie – Cullen **8 (13)**
Cullen – Portsoy **6 (10)**
Portsoy – Keith **17 (27)**
Keith – Dufftown **11 (18)**
Dufftown – Rothes **7 (11)**
Rothes – Elgin **10 (16)**

SCENIC ROUTES

The coastal part of this route
is particularly nice as there are
views of the cliffs, beaches
and small settlements with
their little harbours. Inland,
the route goes through more
good arable farming land,
though south of Keith sheep
farming becomes more
important.

2 days – 125 miles (201km)

THE FISHING TRAIL

**Banff ● Macduff ● Crovie ● Rosehearty ● Fraserburgh
Peterhead ● Cruden Bay ● Ellon ● Pitmedden Garden
Oldmeldrum ● Inverurie ● Huntly ● Banff**

Banff's history as a trading centre has left it with a rich legacy of fine buildings, many from the 18th century. The *museum* features displays on the history of the area and also has a good natural history collection.

The old centre of Banff, *The Plainstones*, was where the local outlaw James MacPherson was hanged, probably in 1700. (See Tour 15.) It features the town's old *mercat cross*, the very ornate *Biggar Fountain* and a *cannon* captured at Sevastopol during the Crimean War. The early 18th-century *Duff House*, which lies close to the town, is one of the finest mansions built by William Adam. It has been described as being in 'extravagant baroque style' and its exterior features a double curving staircase.

About half a mile northwest of Inverurie lies the ancient Brandsbutt Stone, bearing Pictish symbols and an Ogham inscription. Ogham refers to an early British alphabet comprising 20 characters

ⓘ Collie Lodge (seasonal)

*Leave by the **A98** and follow it for a mile (2km) to Macduff.*

Macduff, Grampian

1 This is a busy fishing port and many of the townspeople are connected with some aspect of the industry. There is a weekday fishmarket and boats are built in the local boatyard.

Doune Church has a clock tower of which only three of the four sides have faces. The blank face looks towards neighbouring Banff and was deliberately left like that in response to the hanging of James MacPherson when his last-minute reprieve was on its way. The local people felt so enraged at this miscarriage of justice that they wanted to ensure the people of Banff never knew the correct time again.

*Leave by the **A98** and turn left at the **B9031**. Turn left at the signposted minor road to Crovie, 9 miles (14km).*

Crovie, Grampian

2 Crovie is one of the gems of the northeast. A tiny village of about 40 houses, most of their gable ends face the shore as some form of protection from the furious sea that laps so close to them. There is no road beside the houses so the villagers use wheelbarrows to carry heavy objects along the sea wall from the car-park to their homes.

*Return to the **B9031** and turn left. Follow this road to Rosehearty, 13 miles (21km).*

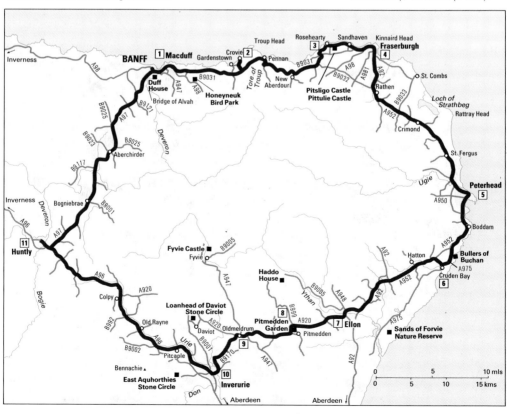

Rosehearty, Grampian

3 Like so many little ports on this coast, Rosehearty's boom time was during the 19th century when over 130 boats fished for herring from here. Such heady days are long gone and many of the local fishermen work out of Fraserburgh.

Just outside the village lie the ruins of **Pitsligo Castle**, a courtyard castle which developed from a 15th-century keep. The building consisted of only three rooms – a kitchen, a dining room and a communal bedroom with 24 beds in it! To its east is **Pittulie Castle**, which dates from the 16th century but was abandoned in the 19th century.

> *Continue on the **B9031** and turn left at the **A98** on the outskirts of Fraserburgh.*

Fraserburgh, Grampian

4 This is one of the busiest fishing ports in the northeast, dealing in whiting, cod, sole, mackerel and herring. The fishmarket is open most days of the week and there is usually something interesting to watch.

The town is built at the promontory of **Kinnaird Head** (which managed to capture the attention of the Egyptian

A decaying sea arch looms up from the shore at Tarlair, near Macduff. Highly-jointed rock is susceptible to the hydraulic action of waves

geographer Ptolemy in the 2nd century AD), and a **castle** was built here at the end of the 16th century; it was later converted into a lighthouse. Close to the castle stands the **Wine Tower**; this rather odd building, which has trap doors instead of an internal staircase, was erected in the 16th century but the use to which it was put is still a mystery.

Saltoun Square, in the centre of the town, has the old **mercat cross** and the **Town House**, which was built in 1855.

ⓘ Saltoun Square

> *Leave by the **A92** then bear left on to the **A952** to Peterhead, 18 miles (29km).*

Peterhead, Grampian

5 This was once Scotland's most important whaling centre until it gave way to the herring industry in 1818. Now Europe's busiest white fish port and the EC's largest fishing port, there is also a lot of commercial

FOR CHILDREN

Good beaches suitable for family outings are not as common as in other parts of this region, but St Combs and Cruden Bay are well worth visiting.

1 *Macduff, Grampian* **Honeyneuk Bird Park**, east of Macduff, is a wildlife and conservation park with many species of birds including owls and various poultry. There are also goats, sheep and pigs, and minority breeds like pot-bellied pigs.

BACK TO NATURE

2 *Crovie, Grampian* South of the charming little village of Pennan, used as the location for the film *Local Hero*, the **Tore of Troup** runs inland for about 8 miles (13km). This deep wooded ravine is very sheltered and is home to badgers, mink, foxes and deer; buzzards may also be seen.

SPECIAL TO ...

This part of Scotland has important crops of granite, and many of the towns and villages on this tour have been built using this distinctive stone. Perhaps the most attractive is Peterhead's, which has large red crystals, quite different from Aberdeen's medium-grained blue-grey rock, or the light grey from Kemnay.

Granite is formed when hot molten rock, called 'magma', cools while still beneath the earth's surface. The colour of the resulting rock depends on the minerals present and the size of the crystal on how slowly the rock cools (the slower, the bigger the crystals).

BACK TO NATURE

7 *Ellon, Grampian* The **Sands of Forvie National Nature Reserve** is a vast dune system that has in the past overwhelmed settlements. It is also home to many birds including arctic terns, Sandwich terns, eider ducks and shelducks. Sea ducks are particularly numerous in the winter, along with divers and grebes.

The Still House at the Glengarioch Distillery, Oldmeldrum

SCENIC ROUTES

On the journey round the coast, there are spectacular views of the cliffs, beaches and sand dune systems. Perhaps the best sections are between Macduff and Fraserburgh and between Peterhead and Cruden Bay.

FOR HISTORY BUFFS

9 *Oldmeldrum, Grampian* **Fyvie Castle**, to the northwest of Oldmeldrum, has undergone many changes from its original 13th-century structure but it has been described as the 'crowning glory of Scottish baronial architecture'. The finest feature inside is the 13-foot (4m) wide stone staircase.

activity connected with supplying the North Sea oil rigs. The Peterhead **lifeboat** is open to visitors. The history of the whaling and fishing industries is told in the local **Arbuthnot Museum**.

ⓘ Broad Street

*Continue on the **A952**, then turn left at the **A975** to enter Cruden Bay.*

Cruden Bay, Grampian

6 This is a popular summer resort with a long sandy beach and a fine golf course. However, visitors may also like to know that the nearby ruins of 17th-century **Slains Castle** are said to have been the inspiration for the novel *Dracula*. The author, Bram Stoker, used to holiday at Cruden Bay and he began writing his famous story here in 1895.

A little further up the coast, the sea has carved deep clefts into the tall cliffs, the most spectacular feature being the **Bullers of Buchan**, a natural arch and a blow hole.

*Leave by the minor road that leads to the **A952**. Turn left at this junction, then turn left again at the **A92**. Turn right at the signposted road to Ellon, 11 miles (18km).*

Ellon, Grampian

7 Ellon was the ancient 'capital' of Buchan, from the time of the Picts up to the defeat of the Norman Comyns who held the land during the Middle Ages. The village gained importance as a crossing point over the River Ythan and its **castle** had a strategically important role to play in defending the district. Apart from the ruins of the old castle, the other historical remains are the **Moot Hill Monument** where there was a motte-and-bailey fort to defend the bridge.

Haddo House, to the northwest of the village, is an imposing mansion built by William Adam in 1732, though much of the interior was redecorated around 1880. The house, which is owned by the NTS, has extensive parklands with walks and an adventure playground.

ⓘ Market Street Car Park

*Leave by the **A920** and follow it to Pitmedden House (a little to the northwest of the village of Pitmedden), 5 miles (8km).*

Pitmedden Garden, Grampian

8 The gardens at Pitmedden were laid out in the 17th century and the formal garden is made up of elaborate geometric designs filled with brilliantly coloured flowers. The **Museum of Farming Life**, in the grounds of the estate, has many exhibits of tools and farm machinery from the past.

The graveyard in **Udny Green**, just south of Pitmedden, contains a rather bizarre little building – a circular **mort house**, built in 1832 to thwart body snatchers. Coffins were placed in here on a turntable, then removed for burial after a maximum stay of three months, the idea being that they would be quite unsuitable for sale by then.

*Continue on the **A920** and join the **A947** to Oldmeldrum.*

Oldmeldrum, Grampian

9 The village retains its medieval street pattern, with the large **Town Hall** dominating the market square. Tucked away on the outskirts of the village is the **Glengarioch Distillery**, on a site said to have had a distillery in 1797. The distilling process consumes a great deal of energy and one rather novel feature of this distillery is that its waste heat is used to grow tomatoes in glasshouses.

To the west of the village lies the little settlement of **Daviot**, just beyond which is the celebrated **Loanhead of Daviot** stone circle. This imposing circle was constructed about 5,000 years ago and perhaps used in viewing the passage of the moon or in various local rites and customs. The most important part of the circle was the huge recumbent boulder which was put into position so that its uppermost face was horizontal. Ten upright boulders were then placed in a circle to complete the structure. The circle was later used for burials and cremations.

*Leave on the **A920** and bear left at the **B9170** to Inverurie, 5 miles (8km).*

Inverurie, Grampian

10 This busy little town is the main shopping and administrative centre for the surrounding district. Its wide main street is dominated by the **Town Hall**, built in Grecian style in 1863.

The town's position at the confluence of the Don and the Urie has given it some importance for a long time and the medieval motte called **The Bass** stands by the River Urie.

West of the town, minor roads lead to **East Aquhorthies stone circle** which has a massive recumbent stone and a circle of smaller uprights.

ⓘ Town Hall, Market Place

*Leave by the **A96** and follow it for 23 miles (37km) to Huntly.*

Huntly, Grampian

11 The long straight main road of this neat little town passes under the arch of the Gordon Schools and heads towards the impressive ruins of **Huntly Castle**, one of the finest castles in this part of the country. A 12th-century Norman motte is still to be seen. Construction of the palace was started beside it in the mid-15th century. The most important decorative features are the carved entrance doorway and the fireplaces. Remarkably, for a roofless building of this age, some of the plasterwork still survives – complete with original graffiti! The castle also had its own prison, a dreadful place formed out of a pit cut deep into the foundations.

ⓘ 7a The Square

*Return eastwards to and continue along the **A96**, then turn left after a short distance at the **A97** to return to Banff.*

Banff – Macduff **1 (2)**
Macduff – Crovie **9 (14)**
Crovie – Rosehearty **13 (21)**
Rosehearty – Fraserburgh **4 (6)**
Fraserburgh – Peterhead **18 (29)**
Peterhead – Cruden Bay **9 (14)**
Cruden Bay – Ellon **11 (18)**
Ellon – Pitmedden Garden **5 (8)**
Pitmedden Garden – Oldmeldrum **6 (10)**
Oldmeldrum – Inverurie **5 (8)**
Inverurie – Huntly **23 (37)**
Huntly – Banff **21 (34)**

Majestic Duff House, Banff. The main block was roofed in 1739, but the planned wings were never built

RECOMMENDED WALKS

Banff, Grampian From **Duff House**, a woodland path leads along the bank of the River Deveron and across the river's gorge via the **Bridge of Alvah**. From there, paths and country roads head towards Macduff and back to Banff.

10 *Inverurie, Grampian* The hill of **Bennachie**, standing to the west of Inverurie, gives outstanding views over the surrounding countryside. The remains of an ancient **hillfort** can be seen near the summit. One popular starting point for the ascent is from a car-park on the northeastern side of the hill and on the way there, look out for the **Maiden Stone**, a 9th-century carved stone that stands by the roadside.

2/3 days – 204 miles (327km)

AROUND THE CAIRNGORMS

Pitlochry ● Killiecrankie ● Blair Atholl ● Dalwhinnie
Kingussie ● Kincraig ● Aviemore ● Cairngorm
Boat of Garten ● Tomintoul ● The Lecht ● Ballater
Braemar ● Pitlochry

Pitlochry is one of the Highlands' most attractive tourist resorts, with its many Victorian hotels and villas dating from the arrival in 1863 of the Perth to Inverness railway.

The town nestles below the hills on the eastern bank of the River Tummel. The river is part of an extensive hydroelectric scheme and the local *dam* and *power station* are worth visiting. Beside the power station, a salmon ladder allows fish to climb upriver to reach their spawning grounds and there is a viewing window through which the salmon can be watched as they make their way upstream between April and October. Close to the salmon ladder stands the beautifully situated *Pitlochry Festival Theatre*. The *Blair Atholl Distillery*, on the town's outskirts was established in 1826. Its attractive blackened and ivy-covered buildings lend an air of rural tranquillity to the production process. It has a visitor centre and tours are available.

> *The Pitlochry salmon ladder wends its way upstream alongside the swirling River Tummel, allowing the fish to safely bypass Loch Faskally Dam and reach their breeding grounds and providing a great attraction for visitors*

More than 600 acres (240 hectares) of this rugged granite country make up the Cairngorm National Nature Reserve – the largest in Britain. Access to a large extent of the area is generally unrestricted

ⓘ 22 Atholl Road

> *Leave Pitlochry by the **A924**, then the **B8019** for about 1½ miles (2km) before turning on to the **B8079** to the National Trust for Scotland Visitor Centre at Killiecrankie, a distance of 4 miles (6km).*

Killiecrankie, Tayside

1 The wooded gorge of Killiecrankie is a strategic pass through the Highlands. A decisive battle was fought near here in 1689 when a Jacobite army defeated a Government force. In the aftermath of the battle, one of the Government soldiers, Donald MacBean, escaped from his pursuers by jumping 18 feet (6m) across the River Garry at a point now known as the 'Soldier's Leap'.

ⓘ NTS Visitor Centre

> *Continue on the **B8079** for 4 miles (6km) to Blair Atholl.*

Blair Atholl, Tayside

2 This little village, situated where the Tilt and Garry rivers meet, is dominated by **Blair Castle**, home of the Dukes of Atholl. The oldest part of the castle, Comyn's Tower, dates back to 1269 but much of the present structure is relatively 'modern'. At the end of the 18th century the castle was completely renovated; parapets and towers were removed and it was turned into a Georgian mansion. The picturesque towers and crow-stepped gables were later additions when the Scots baronial style came into fashion. The castle has extensive grounds with many fine walks. The Duke of Atholl is the only man in Britain to have a private army, a right granted him by Queen Victoria.

> *Leave on the **B8079**, then turn right at the **A9** and head towards Inverness. Bear left at the **A889** and follow to Dalwhinnie, a total distance of 36 miles (57km).*

Dalwhinnie, Highland

3 At an altitude of 1,188 feet (362m), this is the highest village in the Highlands and was an important stopping place in the days when the main highway passed through here. It has a small **distillery** which is open to the public.

*Continue on the **A889** and turn right at the **A86** to Kingussie.*

Kingussie, Highland

4 The main attraction here is the **Highland Folk Museum** and the most fascinating exhibit is the 'black house', built in the manner of the drystone houses that were common on the island of Lewis. Other exhibits bring to life Highland agriculture, the life of the tinkers (travelling people) and the furniture used in Highland houses over the last 300 years.

Across the River Spey stands the gaunt ruin of **Ruthven Barracks** which were built in 1719 but destroyed by the Jacobite army in 1746 to prevent their use by the Hanoverians.

ℹ️ King Street; Ralia, on the A9 near Newtonmore (seasonal)

*Leave by the **B9152** and follow it for 6 miles (10km) to Kincraig.*

Kincraig, Highland

5 The Highland Wildlife Park at Kincraig is home for a collection of animals that once roamed here freely. Reindeer, wild horses, brown bears, wolves, lynx and even bison were at one time native to this part of Scotland. Now they can only be seen from the safety of a car when driving through the park.

The village stands by Loch Insh, which has a watersports centre, while further up the Spey the river widens at

Insh Marshes. This is Scotland's largest inland marsh with a reserve administered by the RSPB (Royal Society for the Protection of Birds), which is particularly good for waders and wildfowl.

*Continue on the **B9152** for 6 miles (10km) to Aviemore.*

Aviemore, Highland

6 Until the 1960s Aviemore was just another small Highland village, but the huge **leisure complex** that was then established has transformed it into the busiest tourist centre in the Highlands. The new buildings sit uneasily in the Highland landscape, but they offer many indoor facilities that are not found elsewhere in the area, hence its popularity, especially with winter visitors who come here to ski in the Cairngorms.

Aviemore has a station on the Perth to Inverness railway line and it is also the southern end of the **Strathspey Railway**; run by enthusiasts, it is based in Boat of Garten.

ℹ️ Grampian Road

Take the Cairngorm road out of Aviemore. Follow it through Coylumbridge, past Loch Morlich and up the mountain road to the Coire Cas ski slopes at Cairngorm.

Cairngorm, Highland

7 The Cairngorm mountains are formed from a massive dissected plateau of granite with an altitude of around 4,000 feet (1,220m). The **chairlift** at Coire Cas is operated throughout the year and climbs to a restaurant near the summit of Cairn Gorm, but it should be remembered that even though it is calm and sunny at the chairlift car-park, it can be very

FOR HISTORY BUFFS

2 *Blair Atholl, Tayside* The two ends of **Glen Tilt** are met during this tour – at Blair Atholl and at Braemar. This was an historically important route across the Highlands but is now the preserve of walkers. In 1861 Queen Victoria passed through it, travelling 69 miles (111km) in one day! Earlier, in the 1840s, the Duke of Atholl attempted to close this right of way and the story of this is celebrated in *The Ballad of Glen Tilt.*

FOR CHILDREN

5 *Kincraig, Highland* The **wildlife park** at Kincraig and the reindeer herd at Cairngorm are worth seeing. There are lots of outdoor activities, both land and water-based, available in the area near Aviemore and the indoor facilities in the town offer useful wet-weather alternatives.

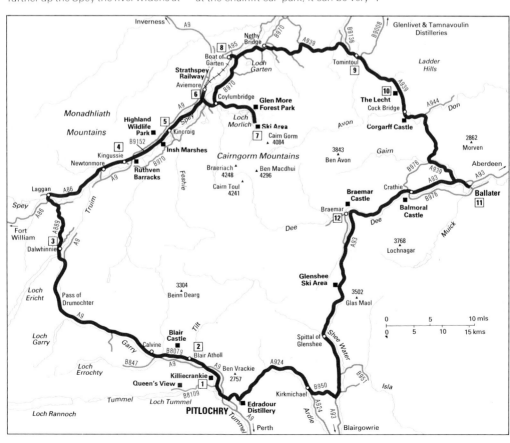

SCENIC ROUTES

The whole of this route offers memorable scenery, but perhaps the most attractive parts are near Blair Atholl, the views of Cairn Gorm and the journey from Donside to Deeside. One very well-known viewpoint just off the route is the **Queen's View**, which is at the eastern end of Loch Tummel.

BACK TO NATURE

4 *Kingussie, Highland* At Kingussie, the **Highland Wildlife Park** gives a good introduction to native mammals and birds that are difficult to see in the wild.

8 *Boat of Garten, Highland* The ospreys at **Loch Garten RSPB reserve** are the most obvious example of how wild animals are being encouraged to re-populate their old haunts. This is assisted by the careful management of the remains of the old Caledonian Forest in the area to the north of Cairn Gorm. Visitors should also look for Scottish crossbills and crested tits in the pine forests, and goldeneye (ducks) and Slavonian grebes on the lochs.

The shrouded form of Loch Morlich backed by the distant Cairngorm mountains. This sandy-shored loch lies at the heart of the Glen More forest park at a height of 1,046 feet (319 m)

windy and bitterly cold near the summit. The Cairngorm plateau is covered with frost-shattered boulders which give little shelter to man or beast, but it does support a herd of reindeer which were introduced here in 1952.

The Rothiemurchus estate and the Glen More Forest Park lie between Aviemore and the Cairngorms and there are many attractive low-level walks through the stands of Scots pine and around Loch Morlich which is a popular watersports centre.

Return to Coylumbridge and turn right at the B970. Follow this towards Boat of Garten and turn left at a signposted unclassified road when the village is neared, 14 miles (23km).

Boat of Garten, Highland

8 The name derives from a chain-operated ferry across the Spey that was replaced in 1899 by a substantial bridge. This is the home of the **Strathspey Railway**, one of the finest tourist attractions in the area, particularly for those nostalgic for the days of steam! The station was originally opened in 1863, and later the line became part of the Highland Railway. Passenger services ceased in 1965.

East of the village stands **Abernethy Forest**, part of the old Caledonian Forest, where there are many splendid Scots pines. Beside Loch Garten, which lies within the forest, is an osprey breeding site and many birdwatchers come each year to witness the progress of the current pair. The

ospreys were hunted out of the Highlands at the end of the 19th century but in the 1950s a nest was found in the district. Today, the RSPB maintains a close guard on the nest and visitors can watch the birds from a covered hide. People who spend some time in the district may be fortunate enough to see an osprey fishing in one of the lochs.

Return along the unclassified road to the B970 and turn left; follow this to Nethy Bridge. Turn right after crossing the River Nethy and follow an unclassified road to the A939. Turn right to reach Tomintoul.

Tomintoul, Grampian

9 This is another of the Highlands' highest villages and its position means that its weather can be rather unpredictable, with snow not unknown in June!

It has a broad main street and a large central square with the local **museum**. Although there are only a few shops, one which will be of interest to many visitors is the well-stocked **Whisky Castle**, which has a vast array of whiskies from many parts of Scotland.

To the north lie two distilleries which offer tours to visitors: the **Glenlivet**, which is famous the world over, and the much more modern **Tamnavoulin**.

i The Square

Continue on the A939 for 7 miles (11km) to the skiing area at The Lecht.

The Lecht, Grampian

10 Just beyond The Lecht stands the imposing **Corgarff Castle**. The loop-holed curtain wall surrounding it was added after the 1745 uprising in order that the Government might use the castle to police this Jacobite area.

Winter visitors should take care if snow is forecast as the Tomintoul to Cock Bridge part of the **A939** is sometimes blocked by winter snow.

*Continue on the **A939** then turn left at the **A93** for Ballater.*

Ballater, Grampian

11 Deeside became fashionable after Queen Victoria built a summer retreat at nearby **Balmoral Castle**. The popularity of 'Royal Deeside' was further increased when the railway line, now closed, was built but it only ventured as far as Ballater as the Queen did not wish her peace and quiet to be disturbed! A small exhibition about the local railway line is housed in the tourist information centre. The town is a good centre from which to explore Deeside, and its solidly built granite houses make it a pleasant place to stroll around.

The present Balmoral Castle was built in 1855 with local granite and is a fine example of the Scots baronial style. It is the Scottish home of the British royal family and the grounds are open to the public when the royal family is not in residence.

[i] Station Square

*Return along the **A93** and continue for 17 miles (27km) to Braemar.*

Braemar, Grampian

12 The village is situated in an important position at the junction of three glens and there have been fortifications here from at least 1390 when **Kindrochit Castle** (now a ruin) was built in what is now the centre of the village. Outside the village, **Braemar Castle** is a good example of a Hanoverian fort which was used to

police the Highlands. Built in 1628, it is open to the public.

The Jacobite rising of 1715 began here and the **Invercauld Arms Hotel** stands on the site where the standard was raised at the start of the campaign to put a Stuart back on the British throne.

Braemar can be busy at times, but never more so than in September when crowds flock to the local highland games, the **Braemar Gathering**. The royal family are regular visitors and among the most popular events are the bagpipe playing competitions and the tossing of the caber. Sport is not new to the village, and in the 11th century King Malcolm Canmore, who needed a personal messenger, held a race here to find the fastest man.

[i] Balnellan Road

*Continue on the **A93** past the Glenshee skiing area at Cairnwell and turn right at the **B950**. Turn right when the **A924** is met and follow this back to Pitlochry, a total distance of 47 miles (76km).*

Pitlochry – Killiecrankie	**4 (6)**
Killiecrankie – Blair Atholl	**4 (6)**
Blair Atholl – Dalwhinnie	**36 (57)**
Dalwhinnie – Kingussie	**18 (29)**
Kingussie – Kincraig	**6 (10)**
Kincraig – Aviemore	**6 (10)**
Aviemore – Cairngorm	**10 (16)**
Cairngorm – Boat of Garten	**14 (23)**
Boat of Garten – Tomintoul	**18 (29)**
Tomintoul – The Lecht	**7 (11)**
The Lecht – Ballater	**17 (27)**
Ballater – Braemar	**17 (27)**
Braemar – Pitlochry	**47 (76)**

The Clunie Water at Braemar flowing to join the River Dee, north of the village. The stream divides the village into Castleton of Braemar and Auchindryne

2 days – 137 miles (220km)

THE CASTLE TRAIL

Aberdeen ● Stonehaven ● Fettercairn ● Drum Castle
Crathes Castle ● Banchory ● Kincardine O'Neil
Burn o' Vat ● Craigievar Castle ● Alford ● Monymusk
Castle Fraser ● Aberdeen

Aberdeen's greatest asset, apart from its position between the two great rivers of the Don and the Dee, is its granite. This grey, hard-wearing stone has been used to build houses and grand public buildings and in the making of the humble street cobble. In recent years the city has gained a reputation for its flowers. To discover its best floral displays, stroll through *Duthie Park* and visit the glass-houses in its *Winter Gardens*.

Old Aberdeen, where the oldest part of the university, *King's College*, and *St Machar's Cathedral* are to be found, has many buildings dating back to medieval times. Beyond the handsome twin-spired cathedral lies *Seaton Park* and the grand *Brig o' Balgownie*, a 14th-century bridge in Gothic style that spans the River Don. *Marischal College*, which is near the city centre, is the world's second largest granite building.

The city has a wide variety of galleries and museums including the *Art Gallery*, the 17th-century *Provost Skene's House* and the cosmopolitan and highly regarded *Maritime Museum*, which is housed in Aberdeen's oldest surviving building.

Top left: A flush of colour amid the tropical glasshouses of the Winter Gardens in the Duthie Park, Aberdeen

ℹ St Nicholas House, Broad Street

*Leave by the **A92** and turn left at the minor road that leads to Stonehaven, 15 miles (24km).*

Stonehaven, Grampian

1 As well as being a port with a long-established harbour, Stonehaven also has the beaches and other facilities that attract many visitors. The oldest part of the town has a 16th-century **Tolbooth** which is now used as a museum with special emphasis on local history and the fishing industry. Above the town, the war memorial stands on a hilltop which offers fine views of the coast and the countryside.

The Scots are well renowned for their celebrations at Hogmanay and Stonehaven celebrates the close of the old year with its **Fireball Festival**. The 'ceremony' may stem from ancient pagan rites, and as the Town House bells strike midnight, the participants march up High Street twirling burning balls of rags and twigs round their heads.

To the south of the town is **Dunnottar Castle**, a 14th-century building on a site fortified since the 5th century. The castle stands on a dramatically positioned headland and in 1651 to 1652 it was able to withstand eight months of siege by Cromwell's army before having to surrender. It was also the place where Scotland's regalia was hidden from Cromwell.

The towering baronial elegance of Crathes Castle competes for grandeur with the equally splendid gardens. The castle's south front developed from the fortifications of war

i Allardice Street

*Leave by the **A957**, turn right on
to the **A92**, then left on to the
A94 southwards. After 7 miles
(11km) turn right at the **B966** to
Fettercairn.*

Fettercairn, Grampian

2 The older houses in this little village
are built from a red-coloured sandstone, much warmer-looking than the
rather austere grey of the granites so
common around the Aberdeen area.
The **mercat cross** stands in the village
square and this dates back to 1670. In
comparison to this traditional piece of
local architecture, a large and very
ostentatious Gothic arch celebrates a
visit by Queen Victoria in 1861.

Fettercairn Distillery stands on the
village outskirts and tours round it are
available. The original building was
established in 1820.

To the north stands the estate of
Fasque, which is open to the public.
This was the home of William
Gladstone, four times Prime Minister.
Many of the rooms have changed
little since the house was built in the
1820s and there is a wealth of
Victorian artefacts, especially in the
kitchens.

*Leave by the **B974** on the Cairn
o' Mount road and head towards
Banchory. Just before the town,
turn right at a minor road (to
Kirton of Durris) and follow this
along the southern bank of the
River Dee. Turn left at the **A957**
to reach Crathes. Turn right at
the **A93** and then left at an
unclassified road to Drum Castle,
a distance of 26 miles (42km).*

Drum Castle, Grampian

3 The old **Tower of Drum** was built in
the 13th century with walls 12 feet
(4m) thick. Beside it stands a relatively 'modern' 17th-century house
which has particularly interesting
domestic rooms. The buildings stand

*A substantial harbour fronts the
fishing port of Stonehaven, while
18th- and 19th-century buildings
line the foreshore. The new half of
the town is separated from the older
port by the Carron Water*

in the Old Wood of Drum, a remnant
of the ancient Caledonian Forest, and
many large oaks, pines and wild
cherry trees still flourish here.

*Return to the **A93** and turn right.
Turn right at the entrance to
Crathes Castle, a distance of
6 miles (10km).*

Crathes Castle, Grampian

4 This L-plan tower-house was built
in the 16th century and contains
fine interior decoration. The painted
ceilings are exceptionally fine – these
date from the late 16th century and
very early 17th century and feature
ancient heroes such as Hector,
Alexander the Great and King Arthur.

The gardens, set within yew hedges
that are about 300 years old, have
excellent examples of the art of
topiary.

*Continue on the **A93** for 3 miles
(5km) to Banchory.*

Banchory, Grampian

5 Situated at the confluence of the
River Dee and the Water of Feugh,
Banchory is a pleasant little highland
town that is a good base from which
to explore the area. Close to the
village, the **Bridge of Feugh** spans a
little gorge and this is a popular place
to watch salmon on their way
upstream. The former Council
Chambers has a small display of local
material.

This is good farming country and
numerous old farm buildings survive.
One of these, to the west of Banchory,
is the restored 19th-century **wood
turning mill** at Finzean. This was in
use until 1974, then abandoned, but
is now happily refurbished to

SCENIC ROUTES

As the **B974** makes its way over the hills to Banchory, it passes the **Cairn O' Mount**, a massive roadside cairn that has been added to by generations of travellers. The road crosses over a fine heather moor and there is a very wide view from the cairn over the moors and the low-lying land known as the **Howe of the Mearns** towards the sea.

FOR HISTORY BUFFS

8 *Craigievar Castle, Grampian*
To the south of Craigievar Castle lies the village of **Lumphanan**, where Macbeth is said to have been killed, and to its southwest stands the **Peel of Lumphanan**, one of the region's earliest earthworks. It dates from the 13th century and the buildings that were stationed on the mound were protected by a wide ditch.

continue turning wooden buckets, hence its more usual name, the **Bucket Mill.**

i Dee Street Car Park

*Continue on the **A93** for 7 miles (11km) to Kincardine O'Neil.*

Kincardine O'Neil, Grampian

6 This small village gained early importance for its position at the Deeside side of the Cairn O' Mount route, and a ferry crossed the river here, later superseded by a bridge in the 13th century. This is one of Deeside's oldest villages and it has a very fine ruined **church**, built in 1233 as a resting place for travellers.

*Continue on the **A93** and turn right at the **B9119**. Turn left at the car-park for the Burn o' Vat.*

Burn o' Vat, Grampian

7 The area around the Vat has been laid out with paths to guide visitors round the many examples showing how the landscape was formed during the Ice Age, about 12,000 to 15,000 years ago.

Huge rivers and streams carried vast quantities of rock debris down from the ice-covered mountains and as they did so, carved out gullies and gorges and dumped the debris on the low-lying land to the east. The Burn o' Vat itself is a huge bottle-shaped pot-hole that was worn out of the solid rock by the rushing water. It is some 65 feet (20m) in diameter, and its base is filled with sand and gravel.

Lochs Davan and Kinord lie to the east of the Vat. These are 'kettle holes', formed where huge stranded blocks of ice eventually melted. There are a number of pleasant walks round Loch Kinord and on the northern shore of the loch is the **Kinord cross-slab**, a 9th-century granite Celtic cross.

The district known as **Cromar**, which lies to the north and east of the Vat has numerous monuments that indicate its occupation by ancient peoples over a long time. One unusual structure is the **Culsh Souterrain** which was found at **Culsh Farm**, on the B9119, after Tarland. This was probably a storehouse built over 2,000 years ago.

*Continue on the **B9119** heading northeast. Turn left at the **A980** in order to reach Craigievar Castle, 15 miles (24km).*

Craigievar Castle, Grampian

8 This castle, built in 1626, has many features that have been untouched since their creation, preserving fine examples of early 17th-century design and workmanship. Built in Scots baronial style, the castle rises six storeys and is topped by turrets, towers and crow-stepped gables. The Great Hall, with its fine plasterwork above the fireplace, is probably the castle's most outstanding piece of internal decoration.

*Continue on the **A980**, then turn right on to the **A944** which leads to Alford.*

Alford, Grampian

9 This is the home of the **Grampian Transport Museum** where visitors can enjoy such diverse exhibits as horse-drawn vehicles, vintage cars, a road roller and even a huge snow plough. One very unusual vehicle is the steam-driven car called the 'Craigievar Express', built by the local postman at Craigievar in 1895. It has three wheels and he used it to carry the post on his round.

The village was the terminus of a railway line from Aberdeen and the former station of the Great Northern Scottish Railway now houses a

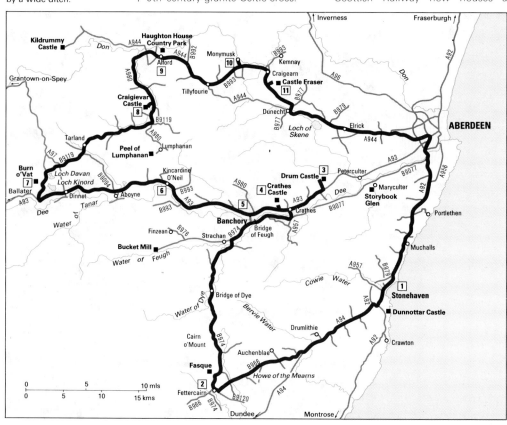

museum. A narrow-gauge railway runs to **Haughton House Country Park** and **Murray Park**. Alford's former cattle market has been preserved and now houses a **rural life museum**.

The great medieval castle of **Kildrummy** lies to the west of Alford near the River Don. This was once one of the North's most important castles and, although now in ruins, many of its surrounding walls still stand. It survived numerous sieges but in 1306, when Robert the Bruce's brother was defending it against English attack, he was betrayed by a smith named Osbarn. Legend has it the gold he was promised for his treachery was poured down his throat, molten!

ℹ️ Railway Museum, Station Yard

*Continue on the **A944** and turn left at the **B993**. Turn left at an unclassified road to Monymusk.*

Monymusk, Grampian

10 This quiet little village, sited just off the main road, has a splendid Norman **church** dating back to the 12th century, when an Augustine priory was also built. The village is laid out very neatly in the fashion of a planned 'estate village', with a little grassy area in its centre.

A former **toll house** stands at the junction of the B993 and the road into the village.

*Return to the **B993** and turn left. Turn right at a minor road to Craigearn, then right again to Castle Fraser.*

The 18th-century Bridge of Feugh spans the turbulent waters of the River Feugh as they rush to merge with the River Dee. An observation platform allows visitors to watch the salmon leaping the rapids

Castle Fraser, Grampian

11 The castle, topped with the usual turrets and towers of the Scots baronial style, was started as a rectangular tower in the mid-15th century. Later additions and alterations transformed it into a handsome mansion house. The **Round Tower** gives an excellent view of the rest of the building and in particular all the different designs of small towers that decorate the upper part of the building. The estate gardens are very pleasant and well worth visiting.

*Turn left after leaving the castle grounds and follow the unclassified road to the **B977** where a right turn is taken. Turn left at the **A944** and return to Aberdeen, 15 miles (24km).*

Aberdeen – Stonehaven **15 (24)**
Stonehaven – Fettercairn **17 (27)**
Fettercairn – Drum Castle **26 (42)**
Drum Castle – Crathes Castle **6 (10)**
Crathes Castle – Banchory **3 (5)**
Banchory – Kincardine O'Neil **7 (11)**
Kincardine O'Neil – Burn o' Vat **12 (20)**
Burn o' Vat – Craigievar Castle **15 (24)**
Craigievar Castle – Alford **8 (13)**
Alford – Monymusk **9 (14)**
Monymusk – Castle Fraser **4 (6)**
Castle Fraser – Aberdeen **15 (24)**

RECOMMENDED WALKS

There are many popular walks in this area and most tourist information centres have leaflets with information on walks, including forest walks, in their area. Places of particular interest include Burn o' Vat, **Haughton House Country Park** and the **West Gordon Way** (which passes near Alford).

THE HIGHLANDS & ISLANDS

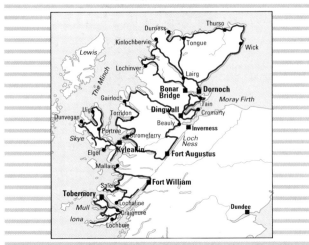

N owhere else in Britain can match the Scottish Highlands and Islands for sheer splendour. The grand mountains, heather-clad hillsides and indented coastline (complete with some of Britain's best beaches) make this classic touring country.

The west coast, with its long broken coastline, provides the most dramatic scenery. Communities are few in number and far apart in some districts, leaving the land to sheep, cattle and midges (these ferocious insects can never be ignored!). The east coast and the Great Glen are more populated and offer better facilities.

This historic region abounds with tales and legends of saints and Picts, of Viking invaders and endlessly warring native clans. It is a long history, much of it bloodied with battles, and it has left the countryside rich in antiquities, and burial chambers, standing stones, brochs, forts and castles which can be seen wherever people found land to settle.

However, in the last 200 years, the proportion of Scots living in the Highlands and Islands has more than halved. Many people have been forced off the land, as during the infamous Highland Clearances which spanned the mid-18th to the late 19th century, when landowners chose to evict their tenants, destroy their homes, and turn the land over to more profitably exploitable tenants – sheep. Many joined the population drift to the Central Belt of Scotland where work was to be found. But many Highland communities are now finding that their population is rising again, as more 'incomers' discover the high quality of life so desperately lacking elsewhere.

Visitors will find that certain events in Scottish history crop up again and again as they tour round the region. The Highland Clearances, the feuding between the clans, the Jacobite Uprising of 1745, the boom and slump of the herring industry: these and many other landmarks in Scotland's history shaped the country and have been well recorded in numerous monuments, both large and small.

Above all, it is the people that make up the country and those that live and work in the Highlands and Islands are having to adapt to great changes. Many rely on the land to make a living and there are still numerous crofting communities. However, new skills are being learned, new trades taken up and new visitors welcomed to the delights of this part of Scotland.

Tour 19

West of the Highland 'gateway' of Fort William, great fingers of land stick out into the sea. These peninsulas, such as Ardnamurchan and Morvern, have scattered crofting communities that are linked by narrow twisting roads offering new views round every corner. Road conditions dictate that progress will not be fast, but then that is no drawback when travelling through one of the least visited parts of the mainland, where each bay and glen is worthy of exploration.

Tour 20

The length of this tour reflects the paucity of major cross-country routes in the Highlands and the extent to which the sea lochs bite into the west coast. This is the Highlands at its best, with giant mountains providing the backdrop to some unforgettable beaches. Inland, the Great Glen lies in a wide gash in the fabric of the land and this cross-country route had been followed over the millennia by settlers, hunters, missionaries, soldiers – and even sailors!

The tumbling Falls of Measach plunge 150 feet (46m) down into Corrieshalloch Gorge

Tour 21

Two cross-country routes link the eastern village of Bonar Bridge with more dramatic west coast scenery. Europe has few wildernesses left, but as visitors approach the uninhabited moor and mountain area of Inverpolly, they can get some feeling of just how starkly beautiful (and inhospitable!) the Highland landscape can be. However, the rich harvest from the sea provides many communities with a good livelihood and helps maintain the Highland crofting traditions.

Tour 22

Much of this long tour around the top of Scotland follows the narrow populated coastal fringe. There seems to be almost no limit to the number of beautiful sandy beaches to be found here, and many of them will be deserted. Caithness, set in a much gentler landscape than Sutherland, has something of a timeless quality about it, especially in the farming areas, and it is rich in prehistoric antiquities that still puzzle the archaeologists.

Tour 23

In many ways, Easter Ross and the Black Isle are very different from the rest of the region. This is particularly good farming country, with large prosperous farms and bustling towns. The blend of gentler Highland landscape with the facilities of seaside resorts makes this district popular with families and those seeking a relaxed tour through pleasant countryside.

Tour 24

Skye, the 'Misty Isle', draws visitors to its shores eager to see the rugged grandeur of the Cuillin Hills and to experience a place where time seems to pass more slowly than on the mainland. The island is so steeped in tradition and history that it lures visitors back again and again.

Tour 25

With its interior composed largely of mountain, moorland and bog, Mull's coastline roads link villages, harbours, farms and castles. The sea is never far away, and with a coastline some 300 miles (480km) long the views towards the sea are as fine as they are varied.

Delicately flowered cottage gardens conceal the harsher aspects of living in the crofting and fishing village of Scourie on the northwest coast

THE ROAD TO THE ISLES

Fort William ● Banavie ● Glenfinnan ● Loch nan Uamh
Arisaig ● Morar ● Mallaig ● Kinlochmoidart ● Acharacle
Glenmore ● Kilchoan ● Strontian ● Lochaline
Ardgour ● Fort William

Little remains of the old fort at Fort William, which was built in 1615 by General Monk. Although many visitors to the Highlands spend some time in the town, it is more of a centre for shopping and services than a tourist resort like Oban. However, the *West Highland Museum*, one of the Highlands' finest museums, has a wealth of material on local history and especially on Prince Charles Edward Stuart ('Bonnie Prince Charlie') and his ill-fated attempt to recapture the British throne for the Stuarts.

Ben Nevis, Britain's highest mountain at 4,406 feet (1,344m), is hidden from the town but good views are obtained further northwards along the *A82*. It is not Scotland's best-looking mountain, but attracts many people. For more information on the mountain, visit the *Scottish Crafts and Ben Nevis Exhibition* in Fort William.

A distinctly Scottish welcome for visiting train passengers to the Highland town of Fort William

ℹ Cameron Square

Leave by the A82 (to Inverness), then turn left at the A830 (to Mallaig). Turn right at the B8004 to the Caledonian Canal's locks at Banavie, 4 miles (6km).

Banavie, Highland

1 Northeast of Fort William, on the way to Banavie, are the impressive, well-preserved ruins of the 13th-century **Inverlochy Castle**, on the banks of the River Lochy. It has massive round towers at the corners and walls 10 feet (3m) thick.

The **Caledonian Canal** runs through the Great Glen from Corpach (just southwest of Banavie) to Inverness, a total distance of 60 miles (97km). It was built between 1803 and 1822 by Thomas Telford so that boats could avoid the treacherous waters round Cape Wrath; the political decision to build the canal was hastened by the government's fear of Napoleon's naval strength. Although some commercial boats still use this beautifully sited waterway, most of the craft on it are motor cruisers or yachts and their passage through the locks is always of interest to landlubbers.

'Neptune's Staircase', the most spectacular part of the canal, is found at Banavie. This is a series of eight locks that raise boats a total height of 64 feet (20m) in a distance of only 1,500 feet (460m).

A short walk along the towpath leads to the basin and sea lock at Corpach; the neat 'pepper pot' **lighthouse** is a delightful structure. From this point there is an excellent view of Loch Linnhe and the surrounding hills. This is probably one of the best places from which to see Ben Nevis.

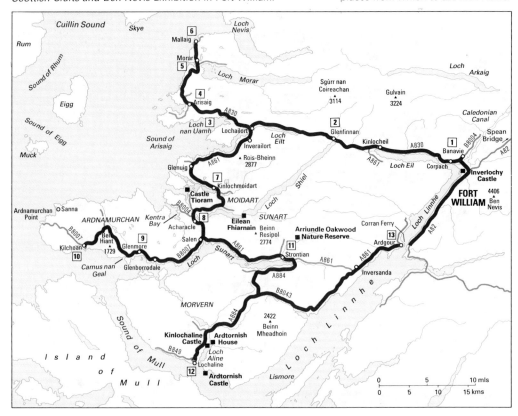

Loch Eilt's ink-blue waters, lying 2 miles (3km) due west of the small village of Glenfinnan on the A830

Glenfinnan, Highland

2 On the fateful afternoon of 19 August 1745, Charles Edward Stuart raised the Stuart standard here and rallied more than a thousand armed supporters to the Jacobite cause. His father was proclaimed King James VIII of Scotland and III of England and Ireland and this historic event started the tragic chain of events known in Scots history as the 'Forty Five'. The army, though initially successful in moving far into England, was eventually defeated at Culloden, near Inverness, on 16 April 1746, a defeat that did much to change the history of Scotland.

The **NTS Visitor Centre** has a good display explaining the events surrounding the arrival of the prince and the raising of the standard. The nearby tall and slender **monument** at the head of Loch Shiel is Scotland's most famous memorial to the Jacobite cause.

The Fort William to Mallaig road runs parallel to the railway line for much of the way. The line's most spectacular structure is the **Glenfinnan Viaduct** with its 21 arches; the local railway station has a little museum depicting the history of the line.

*Return to the **A830**. Turn right and follow the road for 16 miles (26km) to Glenfinnan.*

i NTS Visitor Centre

*Follow the **A830** for 14 miles (23km) to Loch nan Uamh.*

Loch nan Uamh, Highland

3 After the battle of Culloden, Prince Charles made his way back to this area and, on 20 September 1746, he sailed away from this loch on a ship bound for France. The spot from which he sailed is marked by the 'Prince's Cairn'. He had a price of £30,000 on his head but no one betrayed his presence while on the run from government troops, so loyal were the people to the Jacobite cause.

*Continue on the **A830** for 6 miles (10km) to Arisaig.*

Arisaig, Highland

4 This little seaside village has many sandy beaches near by which makes it popular with families in summer. Arisaig has a fine view of the islands of **Rum** and **Eigg** and boats sail from the small harbour to these and other local islands.

*Continue on the **A830** for 6 miles (10km) to Morar.*

Morar, Highland

5 Loch Morar, with a depth of 1,017 feet (310m) is Britain's deepest inland water and the home of Morag, a 'monster' reputed to be related to Loch Ness' Nessie. The loch is a remarkable example of the effect of glaciers during the Ice Age. The ice here was 4,000 feet (1,220m) thick and gouged out the loch's basin to a

8 *Acharacle, Highland* As the
A861 descends to
Acharacle, it passes a minor
road (left) to **Dalelia** and this
leads to a walk to the shores
of Loch Shiel. This is the
narrowest part of the loch and
is almost completely blocked
by **Eilean Fhiarnain** (St
Finnan's Island), where St
Finnan, a disciple of St
Columba, built a **chapel**. The
ruins survive, and legend has
it that a curse has been placed
on anyone daring to remove
the bell Finnan brought from
Ireland. The churchyard was
the burial place of the chiefs
of Clanranald. This was also
the spot from which Charles
Edward Stuart started his
journey up Loch Shiel to
Glenfinnan where he raised
the Stuart standard in 1745.

*A fleet of sea-wearied fishing
vessels rest at anchor within the
calm haven of Mallaig harbour. The
bristling antennae of state-of-the-art
equipment belies the industry's
decline*

depth of more than 1,000 feet (300m)
below sea level.

After tumbling over the **Falls of
Morar**, the River Morar flows over the
Sands of Morar, a wide expanse of
pure white silica sands.

*Continue on the **A830** for
3 miles (5km) to Mallaig.*

Mallaig, Highland

6 Before the arrival of the railway,
Mallaig was a small crofting
community with a few thatched
houses. Today it is the home port of
a substantial fishing fleet and the
mainland terminal for many boats
operating ferry services to the islands.

Day excursions from the harbour
are also available and these give visitors the opportunity to visit Skye or the
'Small Isles' of Eigg, Rum and Canna.

The peninsula of Knoydart is
another fascinating place accessible
by boat. Surrounded on three sides by
sea and on the fourth by mountains, it
is one of Scotland's few wilderness
areas; it retains its character because it
cannot be reached by road. This is
wonderful walking country, where
real peace and quiet can be enjoyed.

The **West Highland Railway** from
Fort William was opened in 1894 in
order to transport the west coast
herring catches to the southern
markets as quickly as possible, and
although the fish-carrying role of the
line has diminished, it is still of vital
economic and social importance to
the area. It is also very popular with

summer visitors, especially when
steam trains are used, and it has been
described as one of the world's most
scenic railway journeys.

*Return along the **A830** to
Lochailort, then turn right at the
A861. Follow this road to
Kinlochmoidart, a total of
31 miles (50km).*

Kinlochmoidart, Highland

7 To the right of the road stand the
'Seven Men of Moidart', a line of
seven beech trees planted early in the
19th century in tribute to the seven
men who landed here with Bonnie
Prince Charlie in 1745.

The area around Loch Moidart is
beautifully wooded with a large
natural oak and birch forest; holly,
cherry and ash are also common.
Today these trees are protected, but in
previous centuries they were used for
charcoal burning or for making lime.
An old **lime kiln** stands opposite the
car-park at the 'Seven Men of
Moidart'.

After climbing out of Kinlochmoidart, look out for a group of four cairns
by the roadside. These are on an old
'coffin route' and mark where coffins
were laid to give their bearers a rest
while carrying their burden over the
trackless hills to the local churchyard.

*Continue on the **A861** for
7 miles (11km) to Acharacle.*

Acharacle, Highland

8 This small village, which makes a
pleasant base from which to explore
the surrounding area, is approached
by crossing the Old Shiel Bridge.

To the west lies **Kentra Bay** with
its fine sandy beaches, and **Castle
Tioram**, a 14th-century castle standing on a tidal island in Loch Moidart.

Though an empty ruin, it was not destroyed in battle, but put to the torch by its owner, the chief of the Clanranalds, during the 1715 Jacobite uprising. He did this to prevent it falling into the hands of his enemies.

*Continue on the **A861** to Salen, then turn right at the **B8007** and follow it to Glenmore.*

Glenmore, Highland

9 Excellent displays on the local land-scape and wildlife can be seen at the **Ardnamurchan Natural History Visitor Centre** here.

Further along the road is the little bay of **Camus nan Geal** beneath the steep slopes of Ben Hiant. In the field at the back of the bay can be found an 18th-century **burial site** and a Bronze Age **standing stone** which has a number of carvings on it; the remains of a small settlement can also be seen here.

*Continue on the **B8007** for 11 miles (18km) to Kilchoan.*

Kilchoan, Highland

10 This little settlement of scattered houses makes a good base for exploring the western end of the Ardnamurchan peninsula; it also has a summer ferry service to Tobermory on the island of Mull. Close to the settlement stands 13th-century **Mingary Castle**. This was originally the seat of the Maclains and later the Campbells of Ardnamurchan, who held it for the king during the Jacobite rising in 1745.

Beyond Kilchoan is **Ardnamurchan Point**, the most westerly point on the British mainland. The view from here encompasses the Inner Hebrides and the islands of Barra and South Uist. Its **lighthouse** was built in the 1840s by Alan Stevenson, one of the three Stevenson brothers who followed their father in designing lighthouses. The building is constructed from pink granite from the Ross of Mull and the design was influenced by Egyptian architecture.

*Return to Salen along the **B8007**, then turn right at the **A861** to Strontian.*

Strontian, Highland

11 The modern portion of this village lies near the main road while the older part is to be found on the western side of Strontian river. From 1722 to 1904, this was the site of mines extracting lead, zinc and silver but the most lasting contribution the village gave to science was through the discovery here in 1764 of the mineral strontianite. The examination of this led to the discovery of the metal element strontium, used in fireworks. Its radioisotope, Strontian 90, is used in nuclear power sources. The old mining area is now a source of barytes which is used in drillers' 'mud' to lubricate the drilling mechanism on North Sea oil rigs.

Distance adds a dreamy haze to the islands of Eigg and Rum, seen across Cuillin Sound

BACK TO NATURE

The grandeur of the scenery derives from the area's fascinating geology, and the most important structure is the Great Glen Fault that runs right through the Highlands along a line joining Fort William and Inverness. Loch Linnhe and the Caledonian Canal lie along this great gash in the earth's surface, produced as the two sides of the glen moved past each other. The very occasional earth tremors indicate that the fault has not yet stopped moving!

SCENIC ROUTES

The '**Road to the Isles**' is the name given to the attractive route from Fort William to Mallaig, which passes through an ever-changing landscape of hills, forest and lochs.

Another outstanding journey is the one along Loch Linnhe, giving good views of Ben Nevis and the hills of Glen Coe.

RECOMMENDED WALKS

There are good walks to be enjoyed in this area and the tourist information centres have guidebooks giving details of many of them. **Glen Nevis**, which is below Ben Nevis and easily reached from Fort William, provides a walk with waterfalls to see on the way. The Caledonian Canal's footpath provides good level walking for families.

Arriundle Oakwood nature reserve lies north of the Strontian river and has fine oaks and Scots pines; a nature trail can be followed through the reserve.

Continue on the A861, then turn right at the A884. Follow this to Loch Aline and then on to the village of Lochaline, 18 miles (29km).

Lochaline, Highland

12 The peaceful Loch Aline, which slices into the broad peninsula of Morvern, seems a rather incongruous place to have a modern mine, but close to the village is a source of very pure silica sand which is used in the production of high quality glassware. Behind the village, in the graveyard of **Keil church**, stands a tall 15th-century Celtic cross, known as the **Morvern Cross**. Lochaline has a ferry service to Fishnish on Mull.

At the head of the loch stand **Kinlochaline Castle** and **Ardtornish House**, which has extensive gardens worth visiting. To the south of the mansion stands 14th-century **Ardtornish Castle**, a prominent building on the coast that is an important landmark to sailors passing through the Sound of Mull.

Arriundle oakwood nature reserve near Strontian. A nature trail allows the visitor to explore the woodland flora and fauna

Return on the A884 to the junction (right) with the B8043. Cars should follow this unclassified road until the A861 is met and then turn right and follow this road to Ardgour. Vehicles pulling caravans should avoid the B8043 and instead continue on the A884 to its junction with the A861; then turn right to Ardgour, a total distance of 30 miles (48km).

Ardgour, Highland

13 The small village of Ardgour has developed at this important crossing over Loch Linnhe. The old jetty here was built by Thomas Telford in 1815, about the same time as the lighthouse.

Take the Corran ferry across Loch Linnhe at the Corran Narrows, then turn left at the A82 and return to Fort William, 8 miles (13km).

Fort William – Banavie **4 (6)**
Banavie – Glenfinnan **16 (26)**
Glenfinnan – Loch nan Uamh **4 (23)**
Loch nan Uamh – Arisaig **6 (10)**
Arisaig – Morar **6 (10)**
Morar – Mallaig **3 (5)**
Mallaig – Kinlochmoidart **31 (50)**
Kinlochmoidart – Acharacle **7 (11)**
Acharacle – Glenmore **12 (19)**
Glenmore – Kilchoan **11 (18)**
Kilchoan – Strontian **29 (47)**
Strontian – Lochaline **18 (29)**
Lochaline – Ardgour **30 (48)**
Ardgour – Fort William **8 (13)**

A freshly landed sea-catch awaiting distribution to the processing plants, restaurants and shops of Scotland

[i] Car Park

*Head southwards on the **A82** for 7 miles (11km) to Invergarry.*

Invergarry, Highland

1 This rather sleepy-looking village was the home of an important clan, the MacDonnells of Glengarry. To the south lie the ruins of **Invergarry Castle**; three castles have stood here, the last one having been burnt in 1746 by Cumberland because Charles Edward Stuart stayed here before and after the battle of Culloden.

Just to the north of Invergarry stands the roadside **Well of Seven Heads**, a gruesome reminder of the slaying of seven MacDonnell brothers who had murdered their dead brother's two sons. The story of this gory event is recorded on a monument inscribed in Gaelic, English, Latin and French.

*Leave by the **A87** (to Kyle of Lochalsh) and follow this for 36 miles (58km) to Shiel Bridge.*

Shiel Bridge, Highland

2 The imposing entry to Shiel Bridge is by the magnificent **Glen Shiel**, on whose north side is the group of mountains known as the **Five Sisters of Kintail**. The mountains are seen to great advantage at **Mam Ratagan**, just a little to the west of Shiel Bridge on the Glenelg road. Like many communities in this region, Shiel Bridge is just a collection of houses at an

English Gothic style at Fort Augustus. The abbey and school occupy the site of the fort that gave the village its name

THE WESTERN HIGHLANDS

Fort Augustus • Invergarry • Shiel Bridge
Kyle of Lochalsh • Plockton • Lochcarron • Applecross
Shieldaig • Torridon • Kinlochewe • Gairloch
Inverewe Gardens • Corrieshalloch Gorge • Strathpeffer
Beauly • Cannich • Drumnadrochit • Fort Augustus

The *fort* built at Fort Augustus by General Wade in 1730 was named after William Augustus, Duke of Cumberland, infamous for his brutal suppression of the Highlanders after the battle of Culloden in 1746. In 1867 the buildings were acquired by Benedictines who used them as their abbey and school; these are now the most prominent structures in the village and are certainly worth seeing as they incorporate many of the fort's interesting buildings such as the *Governor's House*.

Fort Augustus is strategically placed in the middle of the Great Glen and it has become an important centre for visitors cruising on the Caledonian Canal. Forestry is important in the district and there are a number of forest walks near by.

SPECIAL TO...

Many west coast fishing boats bring in prawns and lobsters and local hotels often have wonderfully fresh seafood dishes on their menus. The shellfish, including delicious scallops, are particularly good.

FOR HISTORY BUFFS

2 *Shiel Bridge, Highland* To the west of Shiel Bridge lies the little village of **Glenelg**. The steep and winding road to it (not for caravans!) has long been of strategic importance, hence the 18th-century military road and the (now ruined) **Bernera Barracks** at Glenelg. This route was used by Samuel Johnson and James Boswell in 1773 and their steps are followed by many summer visitors heading towards the Kyle Rhea ferry to Skye.

South of the village stand two Pictish brochs, **Dun Telve** and **Dun Trodden**. When built as defensive structures about 2,000 years ago, they were over 40 feet (13m) high and had stairs and galleries built into their circular walls. These are two of the best preserved brochs in the country.

important junction, in this case at the head of Loch Duich.

Along the northern shore of the loch stands **Eilean Donan Castle**, which dates back to 1220. Shelled by a British frigate in 1719 during an abortive Jacobite rising, it lay in ruins until rebuilding started in 1912. It is now one of the Highlands' most popular castles and is said to be the most photographed castle in Scotland.

There is an NTS centre at **Strath Croe**, to the northeast of Shiel Bridge, with useful wildlife displays explaining the natural history of this wild and beautiful area. A very rough cross-country path from Strath Croe leads to the **Falls of Glomach** where the water of the **Allt a' Ghlomaich** tumbles a total of 750 feet (230m).

i Shiel Bridge; NTS, Strath Croe

*Continue on the **A87** for 15 miles (24km) to Kyle of Lochalsh.*

Kyle of Lochalsh, Highland

3 This bustling industrial village is usually thronged in summer as it is the terminus of the Skye ferry to Kyleakin. Its character may change however, when the bridge to Skye is built.

The western part of this peninsula lies within the NTS's **Balmacara estate**, and one mile (1.5km) after passing the little village of Balmacara, the NTS's **Lochalsh Woodland Garden** is on the left. This boasts a fine collection of mature trees, especially Scots pines, and is developing more exotic species of plants such as bamboo trees.

i Car Park

Leave by the unclassified road that leads northwards for 7 miles (11km) to Plockton.

Plockton, Highland

4 With palm trees growing by the shore of Loch Carron, Plockton exudes the kind of peace and quiet that has attracted generations of painters; indeed, many would regard it as one of the northwest coast's loveliest villages. The sheltered position also provides a much-needed haven for yachts sailing along the west coast.

*Return along the approach road to Plockton and turn left to head eastwards towards Stromeferry, following the shore of Loch Carron. Turn left when the **A890** is met. Follow to just beyond Strathcarron railway station then turn left on to the **A896** to Lochcarron.*

Lochcarron, Highland

5 Lochcarron is essentially a long string of houses (and a few hotels) along the shore of the sea loch. To its south is **Strome Castle**, once a stronghold of the MacDonnells of Glengarry, but destroyed by the MacKenzies in 1602. It commands a fine view of Skye.

Just west of the village is **Loch Kishorn**, a deep and sheltered loch where enormous North Sea oil rigs were once built.

i Main Street

*Continue on the **A896** but turn left at the head of Loch Kishorn*

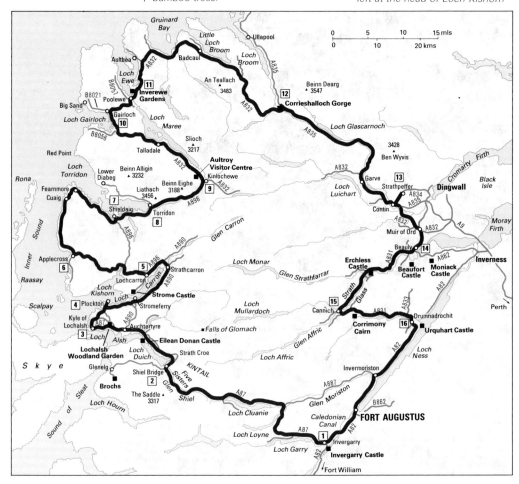

to Applecross. This road is
definitely not for caravans, but
the **A896** from Loch Kishorn to
Shieldaig and the minor road
from Shieldaig to Applecross are
suitable.

Applecross, Highland

6 Applecross was one of the
country's most isolated communities until the coastal road from
Shieldaig was built in the 1970s. The
traditional route, over the 2,053-foot
(626m) pass of **Bealach na Ba** (Pass
of the Cattle), one of the highest roads
in Britain, was a formidable obstacle
to many vehicles and it is often closed
by snow in winter. The zig-zag route
slowly winds up to a wonderful wide
view towards **Kintail**.

An Irish monk, Maelrubha, landed
at Applecross in the AD670s and
founded a monastery which was later
destroyed by Vikings. The local
church has an ancient cross slab 9 feet
(3m) high, with a **Celtic cross**
inscribed. This and others inside the
church may date back to Maelrubha's
time. An old **chapel** stands in the
graveyard and two rounded stones in
front of it mark the traditional resting
place of Maelrubha.

*Head north on the unclassified
road out of Applecross to
Shieldaig. Turn left at the **A896**,
then bear left to enter Shieldaig.*

Shieldaig, Highland

7 This charming village consists of a
row of whitewashed houses standing along the loch's shore. Once
famous for its herring fishing (its
name is Norse for 'herring bay'),
it now relies more on tourism to
maintain its livelihood. Opposite
the harbour lies the small wooded
Shieldaig Island.

*Like a phoenix from its ashes ...
13th-century Eilean Donan Castle.
Defended by a gallant company of
Spanish soldiers during the Jacobite
uprisings, in 1719, HMS Worcester
reduced the great stronghold of the
Macraes to rubble in a matter of
hours*

From around Shieldaig, there are
wonderful views of some of the
Highlands' best scenery. The mountains from Loch Kishorn northwards
to Loch Maree are composed of red
Torridonian sandstone, some 750
million years old. However, around
Shieldaig (and just to the north of it)
the rocks are a highly altered variety
called gneiss which has been eroded
to provide a low, smooth, knobbly
platform above which the giant
Torridon mountains soar.

*Continue on the **A896** for
8 miles (13km) to Torridon.*

Torridon, Highland

8 The houses huddled together in the
village are dwarfed by the mass of
3,456-foot (1,054m) **Liathach**, a
mountain to be attempted only by
experienced walkers as its ridge is
very narrow and exposed. Composed
of Torridonian sandstone, its name
means the Grey One, as four of its
seven tops are composed of the white
rock quartzite.

An **NTS** **countryside centre** is
situated just by the main road and this
has displays and audiovisual presen-
tations on the local geology and
wildlife. Near by, there is a small **Deer
Museum**; deer may be seen near here
or even wandering around the village.

i NTS Centre

*Follow the **A896** for 11 miles
(18km) to Kinlochewe.*

The gigantic, towering peaks of the Torridon Highlands. Torridon village crouches beneath the gullied southern face of Liathach, 'the Grey One', on a debris-cone of frost shattered material

Kinlochewe, Highland

9 This village stands at the head of Loch Maree, which was once called Loch Ewe, hence the name. To its west lies the **Beinn Eighe National Nature Reserve** and the reserve's **Aultroy Visitor Centre** is just along the A832 from the village. Further on is an interesting nature trail which climbs to a fine view over the loch towards **Slioch**, the 3,217-foot (980m) high mountain that dominates the surrounding district.

Loch Maree is one of the country's finest lochs and is steeped in history. The tiny **Isle Maree** was once a sacred place of the Druids, who are said to have introduced oak trees, one of their religious symbols. In the 7th century, St Maelrubha came and set up his cell here and, for similar reasons, planted holly trees. In later centuries, paganism was practised here and rites involving the sacrifice of a bull occurred on the island as late as the 17th century.

The **Loch Maree Hotel** has a large boulder outside it on which is a Gaelic inscription celebrating a visit by Queen Victoria; a translation is above the hotel's entrance.

*Leave Kinlochewe on the **A832** for 20 miles (32km) to Gairloch.*

Gairloch, Highland

10 This widely scattered crofting and fishing community is the district's main centre and it has developed into a popular place for holidays as it combines fine scenery with long stretches of sandy beaches. Fishing is important here and the harbour is well worth visiting when the boats come in. The fishing industry, crofting and other aspects of local life form important displays at the local **Gairloch Heritage Museum** which was developed from a farmstead with a cobbled courtyard.

i Auchtercairn

*Continue on the **A832** for 7 miles (11km) to Inverewe Gardens, just beyond the village of Poolewe.*

Inverewe Gardens, Highland

11 In 1862 Osgood MacKenzie started a long labour of love when he began transforming an area of barren ground here into one of Britain's most remarkable gardens. Conifers were planted to form shelter belts, wet land was drained, soil was carried in on men's backs and in 60 years, the local people had created a garden that gives great pleasure to over 100,000 visitors each year. Inverewe lies at the same latitude as Siberia, but here, bathed by the warm Gulf Stream, it boasts palms, magnolia, hydrangea, rhododendrons and many other beautiful plants.

On a summer's day Loch Ewe is a peaceful place, a far cry from the days of World War II when it was a convoy station for ships bound for Russia or Iceland.

Aultbea (a little further along the road) was the depot's HQ and remains of gun emplacements have been kept as reminders of the district's role in those dangerous days. Look out for information boards near Aultbea's pier.

i NTS Centre

*Continue on the **A832** to the **A835**. Turn left and continue for less than a mile (1.5km).*

Corrieshalloch Gorge, Highland

12 Much of the Highland landscape was sculpted by the movement of ice during the last Ice Age. Often the ice smoothed the land, but at Corrieshalloch Gorge its meltwater flowing down the River Broom gouged out this spectacular rugged gorge about one mile (1.5km) long. A narrow bridge crosses the chasm with the water plunging over the **Falls of Measach** some 150 feet (45m) below – this is not the place for vertigo sufferers! The bridge was built by Sir John Fowler, joint designer of the Forth Rail Bridge, but this is hardly on the same scale and there is a limit to the number of people permitted on the bridge at one time!

The busy fishing port of **Ullapool** lies further down Loch Broom. This bustling little village was founded in 1788 by the British Fisheries Society to take advantage of the huge shoals of herring found in nearby seas. An important ferry terminal for Stornoway; cruises to the Summer Isles are also available from the harbour.

*Head southeast on the **A835** towards Inverness. Turn left at Contin on to the **A834** to Strathpeffer.*

Strathpeffer, Highland

13 Strathpeffer prospered as a spa in the 19th century after springs (four sulphur and one chalybeate) were developed. The Victorian hotels and large villas date from the spa's heyday and today the hotels still do a brisk trade, catering mainly for bus tours. The spa water can be sampled in a small building by the Square but beware – its taste is even more pungent than its smell! Local handicrafts can be bought at the small shops now occupying the old railway station buildings.

At the northern end of the village is the **Eagle Stone**, a Pictish stone also said to celebrate a victory of the Munros over the MacDonalds. To the east, the prominent hill of **Knockfarrel** affords fine views over the district.

i The Square

*Return along the **A834** to the **A835** and turn left. Turn right at the **A832** and at Muir of Ord take the **A862** southwards to Beauly.*

Beauly, Highland

14 Mary, Queen of Scots is supposed to have come here in 1564 and taken a liking to the place; tradition has it she described it as a '*beau lieu*' (beautiful place), hence its name. However, it is more likely Beauly derives from the name given to the 13th-century priory around which the

The close proximity of the Gulf Stream enables the remarkable gardens at Inverewe to grow rare and subtropical plants. Loch Maree lies to the southeast

town was built. **Beauly Priory** was founded in 1230 and the present ruins date from the 13th to the 16th centuries. In 1572 Lord Ruthven obtained royal permission to strip the lead off the roof and by 1633 the building was in a ruinous condition. The town's 'modern' planned layout (built around 1840) features a wide market square and a grid street pattern.

There are a number of castles to be found in the surrounding district. To the southeast is **Moniack Castle**, which makes wine from local produce; to the south is **Beaufort Castle**, built about 1880 in Scots baronial style; and near the road to Cannich stands **Erchless Castle**, a fine building that was described at the end of the 19th century as 'modernised, yet still a stately old pile'.

*Leave on the **A862** (to Inverness) and turn right at the **A831** and continue to Cannich, 17 miles (27km).*

Cannich, Highland

15 Cannich stands at the head of Strathglass, a glen not normally on tourist routes. The lower part of the glen has an impressive narrow gorge (at **An Druim**) and there are a number of hydroelectric power stations here.

To the west of Cannich lie some very beautiful glens – **Glen Affric**,

FOR CHILDREN

10 *Gairloch, Highland*
Gairloch has some of the best beaches in the western Highlands. As well as the beach at the village, there are good ones relatively nearby, at **Big Sand** (to the west) and **Red Point** (further away to the southwest). For wet-weather activity, there is a swimming pool at **Poolewe**. This is one of the few indoor activities for children in the region, something that may have to be considered if the weather is bad.

SCENIC ROUTES

As a detour, the narrow and twisty road from Torridon to Lower Diabeg is highly recommended as there are splendid views of Loch Torridon. In addition, the small picturesque lochside settlements of **Inveralligan** and **Lower Diabeg** are worth seeing.

Glen Cannich and Glen Strathfarrar. These can give good walks as the scenery can be spectacularly wild in places: Scots pines are being regenerated and there are chances of seeing red deer.

Corrimony Cairn is found just off the Cannich to Drumnadrochit road. This is about 4,000 years old and has a central grave chamber which can be reached by crawling through the passageway. Standing stones ring the cairn and the large capstone lying on top of it has small circular indentations called 'cup marks' on it. Further along this narrow road, the standing stone known as **Mony's Stone** can be found, as well as the walled rectangular graveyard of **Clach Churadain** (St Curadan's Cemetery).

*Continue on the **A831** for 12 miles (19km) to Drumnadrochit.*

Drumnadrochit, Highland

16 The district round the village attracts huge numbers of visitors, all here hoping to see one thing – **Nessie**, the Loch Ness monster. The loch is only 2 miles (3km) wide at this point but about 750 feet (230m) deep and many 'sightings' of Nessie have been reported here.

In the AD600s, St Adamnan told how Columba drove back a monster when it was about to attack a swimmer. Since then, there have been many reported appearances and frequent scientific expeditions have attempted to find her, but there is still no definite proof that a monster exists; however, even sceptical visitors should keep a loaded camera handy! **Loch Ness Centre** in Drumnadrochit has exhibits of almost everything connected with Nessie – from explanations of the loch's natural history

The Caledonian Canal enters the southern end of Loch Ness at Fort Augustus. Thomas Telford's great feat of engineering connects the North Sea to the Western Ocean

and equipment used in expeditions to photographs of the beast herself.

Just outside the village stands one of the region's finest ruins, **Urquhart Castle**. The site may have been fortified in the Dark Ages but the present structure dates back to the 13th century. Its commanding position in the Great Glen gave it immense military importance and part of it was blown up in the late 17th century to prevent it falling into the hands of Jacobites.

Further south of the castle, the road passes a **cairn** erected to John Cobb who died on the loch in 1952 while attempting to set up a new world speed record; he achieved the remarkable speed of 206mph (331kph) before the accident.

The village of **Foyers** can be seen on the opposite shore of the loch. In 1896, Britain's first major commercial hydroelectric power station was built here to provide energy for an aluminium works. These buildings can still be seen though the factory has long since closed. Today, a large pump-storage scheme produces electricity using the water of Loch Mhor, which is on the moorland above the village.

*Head south on the **A82** for 18 miles (29km) and return to Fort Augustus.*

Fort Augustus – Invergarry **7 (11)**
Invergarry – Shiel Bridge **36 (58)**
Shiel Bridge – Kyle of Lochalsh **15 (24)**
Kyle of Lochalsh – Plockton **7 (11)**
Plockton – Lochcarron **19 (31)**
Lochcarron – Applecross **18 (29)**
Applecross – Shieldaig **26 (42)**
Shieldaig – Torridon **8 (13)**
Torridon – Kinlochewe **11 (18)**
Kinlochewe – Gairloch **20 (32)**
Gairloch – Inverewe Gardens **7 (11)**
Inverewe Gardens – Corrieshalloch Gorge **39 (63)**
Corrieshalloch Gorge – Strathpeffer **29 (47)**
Strathpeffer – Beauly **12 (19)**
Beauly – Cannich **17 (27)**
Cannich – Drumnadrochit **12 (19)**
Drumnadrochit – Fort Augustus **18 (29)**

A barricade of empty, wooden fish boxes at Lochinver. The town is the home port to a commercial fishing fleet, an angling centre and the base for boat trips to the islands of Enard Bay

ⓘ Bonar Bridge

*Leave by the **A836** and turn left at the **A837**. Continue on this to the Ledmore Junction, then turn left onto the **A835** to the Nature Trail at Knockan Cliff.*

Knockan Cliff, Highland

1 The geological trail at Knockan Cliff provides a wonderful view of the district's unique landscape. Tall and isolated sandstone mountains rise steeply from the boggy moorland which is based on the very old rock known as Lewisian gneiss. This wilderness is part of the **Inverpolly National Nature Reserve** and its visitor centre gives an invaluable introduction to this strange and fascinating landscape. The walks are spectacular, but only for prepared and experienced walkers. At one point on the trail, you can stand beside the world-famous **Moine Thrust** where a huge slab of land (running from Loch Eriboll on the north coast all the way to the island of Islay) moved many miles westward. As a result of this, geologically 'older' rock now lies above the 'younger' rock, quite contrary to the normal succession of rocks.

Much of Inverpolly is covered with wet heath, its main plants being heather, cottongrass and deergrass. The myriad boggy areas and little pools give shelter to bog myrtle and unusual plants such as the carnivorous sundew. Deer roam the land, spending summer in the high corries, but moving down to sheltered places

THE WILD WEST

Bonar Bridge ● Knockan Cliff ● Inchnadamph
Lochinver ● Kylesku ● Scourie ● Kinlochbervie
Lairg ● Bonar Bridge

Bonar Bridge was named after the first bridge to be built over the Kyle of Sutherland at this point, designed by Thomas Telford but later destroyed by a flood, with the loss of over 100 lives. The present structure is the third to have crossed this important stretch of water and a pedestal at the village end of the bridge gives information on all three bridges.

The village of *Ardgay*, which stands on the other side of the bridge, was once the site of important cattle markets, especially in the 19th century. A huge white quartzite boulder, the *Clach Eiteag*, stands by the roadside and this was moved from place to place up until the 1930s to mark the spot where the year's market was to be held. Look out for a substantial *ice-house* on the landward side of the Bonar Bridge to Ardgay road. *Carbisdale Castle*, perhaps Scotland's grandest youth hostel, stands further up the Kyle. This was built between 1906 and 1917 for a Duchess of Sutherland.

FOR HISTORY BUFFS

Bonar Bridge, Highland To the west of Bonar Bridge, a narrow road leads through Strathcarron to **Croik Church**. This was built by Thomas Telford in 1827 for what was then a well-populated district. But, in 1845, in the terrible days of the Clearances, the landowner tried to evict the people as sheep were more profitable 'tenants'. Three attempts were made to throw the 18 families out of their homes and eventually they were forced to gather at this church with only a few possessions. They stayed there for a week, sheltering under rough tents made of blankets and recorded their plight by scratching messages on the church's window panes.

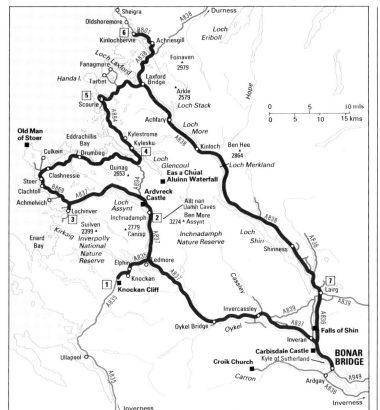

RECOMMENDED WALKS

3 *Lochinver, Highland* To the south of Lochinver, a path follows the River Kirkaig to the **Falls of Kirkaig**; further on, at **Fionn Loch**, there is a very good view of Suilven.

6 *Kinlochbervie, Highland* One of the 'classic' walks in the region is to **Sandwood Bay**, the path to which starts at **Blairmore** between Oldshoremore and Sheigra. Sandwood Bay has a ghost – a 'bearded sailor' – and mermaids are said to have been seen here!

There are also forest walks in many places, such as the **Falls of Shin** and at **Carbisdale Castle**.

during the winter. Otters, wild cats, pine martens and badgers can also be seen in the district. In good weather, this is the Highlands at its best; in bad weather, you won't see anything!

Return along the A835 to the Ledmore Junction. Turn left at the A837 and follow this to Inchnadamph, 11 miles (18km).

Inchnadamph, Highland

2 A hotel and a few houses stand near the road at the **Inchnadamph Nature Reserve**, in an area popular with anglers. This is limestone country and the **Allt nan Uamh caves** on the valley of the River Traligill were used by late Stone Age people. Some of the earliest traces of people living in Scotland have been found here, presumably attracted by better soil and the 'ready-made' houses.

Near the roadside houses, a cairn stands as a memorial to the two geologists, Benjamin Peach and John Horne, who unravelled the mysteries of the local landscape.

Beyond the settlement lies **Loch Assynt**, its pine-clad islands standing in stark contrast to the grassy hillsides. By its shore stands the ruin of **Ardvreck Castle**. In 1650 the Marquis of Montrose (well-known for his exploits against the Covenanters, religious dissenters) fled here. Neil Macleod imprisoned him and dispatched him to Edinburgh to be barbarously hanged, drawn and quartered. Although Macleod expected a bounty of £20,000 for Montrose, he was paid in oatmeal – 56,000 pounds (25,000kg) of it!

Calda House, which stands near the castle, was built in 1695 but was burned down in mysterious circumstances in 1737.

Continue on the A837 for 13 miles (21km) to Lochinver.

Loch Assynt from Inchnadamph. It is the 6-mile (10km) remnant of a more horseshoe-shaped loch that gradually silted up

Lochinver, Highland

3 This is Assynt's main village and an important fishing port specialising in white fish and shellfish.

During the summer it is popular with visitors, walkers and fishermen. A local place of interest is the **Highland stoneware factory**, which produces many types of high quality hand-painted pottery.

From north of Lochinver, there are magnificent views of **Suilven**, at 2,399 feet (731m), one of Britain's most spectacularly shaped mountains. From this direction it rises as a huge dome of reddish-brown sandstone above the platform of the much lighter-coloured gneiss. The Vikings called it Sul Fhal, the Pillar Mountain, but the Gaelic name is Caisteal Liath, the Grey Castle. The summit sometimes holds snow until midsummer, and when the MacKenzie Earls of Cromartie first held it for the Crown in the 17th century, part of the rent was a bucket of snow whenever demanded.

ℹ️ Main Street

Leave by the A837 and turn left at the B869. Continue on this road to the A894, then turn left to reach the bridge at Kylesku. The B869 is a narrow twisting road with many steep hills and it is unsuitable for caravans. An alternative route for caravans is the A837 from Lochinver to Skiag Bridge and then left at the A894.

Kylesku, Highland

4 The Kylesku bridge, a graceful concrete construction that has won many accolades, crosses Loch a' Chàirn Bhain with a view towards the pointed peak of **Quinag** which dominates the southern shore. To the east, the loch splits into two arms and boat trips are available on **Loch Glencoul** to visit seals and herons and to get a view of the remote waterfall **Eas a Chùal Aluinn**. This is Britain's highest waterfall and it is over 650 feet (200m) high.

The car park on the northern side of the bridge offers excellent views of Quinag, the huge mountain that lies between Kylesku and Loch Assynt. It has seven peaks, the highest being 2,653 feet (808m). Like many of the neighbouring hills, it has a base of gneiss, but for the most part is sandstone; a few of the peaks have quartzite caps. Its name comes from the Gaelic *Cuinneag*, meaning a churn or pail.

*Continue on the **A894** for
12 miles (19km) to Scourie.*

Scourie, Highland

5 This crofting community nestles comfortably in a sheltered hollow. It is a popular centre from which to tour the district and many walkers, fishermen and other visitors find this a charming base. Despite its northerly position, palm trees grow in the garden of **Scourie Lodge**.

Becalmed Atlantic breakers whiting the shore around Scourie Bay

The local landscape has earned the description 'knob and lochan', (a lochan is a small loch) as the undulating gneiss landscape is studded with little hillocks and countless pools. Where peat bogs have developed, these are used as a source of fuel and many of the villagers spend time during the early summer cutting the peats and stacking them to dry before taking them home for the winter.

To the north, **Loch Laxford** is a haven for seabirds and seals. Summer cruises on the loch are available from **Fanagmore**.

*Continue on the **A894** to Laxford
Bridge and turn left at the **A838**.
Turn left at the **B801** which ends
at Kinlochbervie, a distance of
16 miles (26km).*

Fishing is one of the west coast's most important industries. Lochinver is a busy port and Kinlochbervie is now Britain's third biggest white fish port. Local restaurants will normally have fresh seafood on the menu as well as locally caught salmon and trout.

The RSPB's Handa Island lies a mile off the coast, north of Scourie and can be reached by boat from the tiny village of Tarbet. The island's many birds have been protected since 1962

Kinlochbervie, Highland

6 In the 1960s this crofting village began its transformation into one of Scotland's most important modern harbours. Now many boats, a large proportion of them originally from the more traditional fishing ports of the east coast, land substantial catches of cod, haddock, whiting and other varieties.

The minor road beyond Kinlochbervie leads to the little community of **Sheigra**, passing glorious coastal scenery at crofting townships such as **Oldshoremore** (where there is a superb beach). The 13th-century manuscript of the Haakon Saga records that King Haakon anchored at Oldshoremore in 1263 at the start of his invasion of Scotland.

The view to the east is dominated by the great hills of **Ben Stack**, **Arkle** and **Foinaven**. Until recently, 'Munro baggers' (hillwalkers 'collecting' hills of over 3,000 feet (914m) high to add to their list of conquests) left Foinaven alone as it was reckoned to be only 2,980 feet (908m). But recent

measurements now put it at 3,002.6 feet (915m).

*Return along the **B801** and the **A838** to Laxford Bridge and turn left. Continue on the **A838**, then turn right at the **A836** to reach Lairg, 46 miles (74km).*

Lairg, Highland

7 Lairg was established beside the River Shin in one of the few areas of decent arable land in Sutherland. This district was once quite well populated, but after the Clearances many of the displaced people emigrated to America or the British colonies.

Further down the river are the **Falls of Shin**. This is a good salmon river and fish must climb the falls in order to return to their spawning grounds upstream. In days of old, poachers used to come to the falls and either spear or shoot the fish as they attempted to leap the falls.

*Leave by the **A836** and follow it for 11 miles (18km) back to Bonar Bridge.*

Bonar Bridge – Knockan Cliff **36 (58)**
Knockan Cliff – Inchnadamph **11 (18)**
Inchnadamph – Lochinver **13 (21)**
Lochinver – Kylesku **27 (43)**
Kylesku – Scourie **12 (19)**
Scourie – Kinlochbervie **16 (26)**
Kinlochbervie – Lairg **46 (74)**
Lairg – Bonar Bridge **11 (18)**

Hardy Scrabster fishermen haul ashore crates of iced-fish, the productive results of a day's hard labour at sea

NORTHERN HIGHLIGHTS

Dornoch ● Tongue ● Loch Eriboll ● Durness ● Bettyhill
Reay ● Thurso ● John o' Groats ● Wick
Hill o' Many Stones ● Dunbeath ● Helmsdale ● Brora
Golspie ● Dornoch

i The Square

*Leave by the **A949** and turn right when the **A9** is met. Turn left at the **A839** and follow it to Lairg. Leave Lairg by the **A836** and follow it to Tongue, 59 miles (95km).*

Tongue, Highland

1 Tongue occupies a marvellous position overlooking the wide sandy estuary of the Kyle of Tongue. To the west of the village stands the ruin of **Castle Varrich**, or Caisteal Bharraich, a 14th-century stronghold of the MacKays on a site that may have been used by an 11th-century Norse king. Nearby **Tongue House** used to be the home of the chiefs of the MacKay clan.

*Leave by the **A838** and follow it for 12 miles (19km) to Loch Eriboll.*

Loch Eriboll, Highland

2 This is one of the north coast's deepest and most sheltered sea lochs and it was used during World War II by convoys of ships waiting to sail across the North Atlantic. The sailors knew this rather desolate place as 'Loch 'Orrible'!

On the eastern side of the loch, a spit runs out to the rocky promontory of **Ard Neackie** on which are the very substantial remains of four **lime kilns** which were constructed around 1870.

*Continue on the **A838** for 19 miles (31km) to Durness.*

Dornoch is a popular holiday resort, with fine beaches and a championship golf course. Its attractiveness is enhanced by its sandstone buildings and a spacious centre dominated by the *cathedral*. Construction of the cathedral began in the 13th century, but a disastrous fire in 1570 destroyed much of it, leaving only the tower and its spire. Some restoration was undertaken in the 17th century, but the major work was carried out in the mid-18th century and also in 1924, its 700th anniversary. The town's *mercat cross* can be seen beside the cathedral's perimeter wall and inside the burial ground lies a *'plaiden ell'*, which was used to measure cloth at medieval fairs held there. The *bishop's castle* is now part of the Dornoch Castle Hotel.

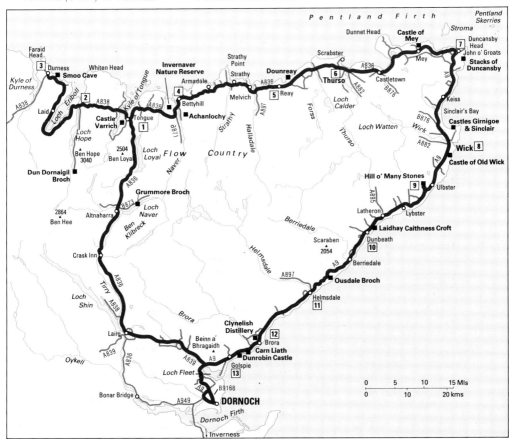

BACK TO NATURE

While the attention of most visitors will be focused on the coast, the landward scenery should not be ignored as the peat bogs from **Loch Loyal** eastward are regarded as being of world importance. This is the 'Flow Country', a wilderness relatively undisturbed by humans for at least 6,000 or more years. This is home to such rarities as the freshwater pearl mussel, insectivorous plants such as the sundew and to birds – including 70 per cent of Europe's breeding population of greenshank. Golden eagles, short-eared owls and peregrines all treat this as their hunting ground. Unfortunately, this beautiful and very desolate region is threatened by intensive forestry, often planted for tax advantages rather than from a wish to grow a worthwhile crop, and a great debate is still continuing on how to preserve this fine example of Scotland's natural heritage for future generations.

Durness, Highland

3 A popular stopping point for visitors, not only for the local scenery, but also for the huge expanses of sandy beaches at the village and at neighbouring Balnakeil.

Durness is situated in a limestone area and is best known for **Smoo Cave**. The main cavern is huge – about 200 feet (60m) long and 110 feet (35m) wide and is easy to enter. Beyond this, a second cave has a 'swallow hole' in its roof and a stream, the **Allt Smoo**, tumbles 80 feet (25m) into it. A third cave can only be entered by boat.

To the west of the village lies the beautiful **Balnakeil Bay** which has a wide sweep of sand backed by tall grass-covered dunes. The site of the ruined **church** nearby may date back to the 8th century when St Maelrubha of Applecross was in this district. The southern wall of the church contains the tomb of the murdered Donald MacLeod, reckoned to be responsible for 18 deaths. It is said that he was so worried that his remains would be dug up after burial by families seeking revenge, he offered a local landowner a huge sum of money to reserve this tomb where he thought his bones might be safe.

In many ways, the **Balnakeil Craft Village** is a memorial to days gone by. It was planned by the Ministry of Defence as an 'early warning station' but by the time it was built the technology was obsolete so the buildings were abandoned. They were subsequently taken up by craftsmen and women and their families who together have built up one of the Highlands' most fascinating communities. Crafts such as marquetry, knitting, pottery and woodturning are represented here and each of the craft

Smoo Cave, Durness. The name is derived from a Norse word smuga *meaning cleft. Inspection shows that it was created partly by an underground river and partly by marine erosion*

shops has a display where the high-quality goods can be viewed.

Cape Wrath can be reached by ferry and bus from the Kyle of Durness. The headland at Cape Wrath, the north-western tip of mainland Britain, rises some 360 feet (110m) from the sea and is topped by a **lighthouse** built by Robert Stevenson, grandfather of Robert Louis Stevenson, in 1828. The area between the cape and the kyle is a vast expanse of peat bog known as the **Parbh** and this comes to an abrupt end at the coast which has the highest cliffs on the mainland, the biggest being **Clo Mor** which is over 600 feet (180m) high.

🛈 Sango, Durness

*Return along the **A838** to Tongue, then follow the **A836** along the coast to Bettyhill.*

Bettyhill, Highland

4 Bettyhill village was founded by people displaced during the Clearances and the name derives from Elizabeth, Countess of Sutherland, wife of the duke who was responsible for many of the region's evictions. The local **Strathnaver Museum** is housed in a church built in 1774 and in the churchyard stands the **Farr Stone**, a good example of early Christian Celtic sculpture. The museum has features on the local clearances as Strathnaver was one of the centres of the evictions. To the south of Bettyhill stand the remains of the clearance village of **Achanlochy**, where seven families were thrown out of their homes.

The village stands close to the River Naver and looks over the sandy **Torrisdale Bay**, on the southern side of which is the **Invernaver Nature Reserve**. Its flora is of an unusual mix as the blown shell-sand has mixed with the otherwise acid soil and supports a wide variety of plants, including dwarf juniper, thrift, alpine bistort and creeping willow.

*Continue on the **A836** for 19 miles (31km) to Reay.*

Reay, Highland

5 The original Reay was buried in sand in the early 18th century, but the village was rebuilt and the local **church** dates from 1839 when the new community was being re-established. Reay has given its name to the 'Reay Country', the great inland tract of deer 'forest', though it should be noted that when the word 'forest' is used to describe a hunting ground, it does not necessarily imply that there are many trees there!

Today, Reay is best known for the hemispherical dome of the nearby nuclear reactor at **Dounreay**. In 1955 construction of the Dounreay Fast Reactor was begun in order to produce electricity. In 1974 a new Prototype Fast Reactor began operating. As well as producing electricity it is involved in much scientific research. Tours round the site are available.

*Continue on the **A836** for 12 miles (19km) to Thurso.*

Thurso, Highland

6 Thurso began as a fishing settlement and the fishermen's houses can be seen above the harbour. However, it developed rapidly in the early 19th century when huge quantities of Caithness 'flags' were exported. These are the flat slabs of local sandstone that were in demand for pavements in the greatly expanding towns and cities of Britain and other countries. The flags are so common that even local fences are made of them.

Today, Thurso has again expanded dramatically as a result of the building of the reactors at Dounreay. However, it still has a number of substantial sandstone buildings and these help to retain its homely character. The 17th-century **Thurso Castle** overlooks the harbour and beyond it **Harold's Tower**, erected over the grave of Earl Harold, the 12th-century ruler whose domain covered parts of Caithness, Orkney and Shetland.

The **Thurso Folk Museum** contains a wide variety of interesting artefacts including the **Ulbster Stone** (a Pictish sculptured stone), and also an important collection of rocks and fossils collected by Robert Dick in the 19th century.

Northeast of Thurso, on the A836, is the village of **Mey**. The **Castle of Mey** is the summer residence of the Queen Mother.

i Riverside

*Continue on the **A836** for 20 miles (32km) to John o' Groats.*

John o' Groats, Highland

7 This is often thought to be mainland Britain's most northerly point, but in fact **Dunnet Head** (to the west) holds that distinction. However, it *is* the country's most northerly village and therefore either the start or finish of the ever popular John o' Groats to Land's End long-distance walks.

The village was named after Jan de Groot, a Dutchman who started a ferry service from here to Orkney in the 16th century. Trips to the Orkney Islands leave from the local harbour.

Near by, **Duncansby Head**, the northeastern tip of the mainland, has

Island pillars of Old Red Sandstone collectively form the Stacks of Duncansby. These magnificent structures have gradually developed during thousands of years of coastal erosion

cliffs 210 feet (64m) high and a lighthouse perches on top of it. With care (it can be very windy!), the cliff tops can be followed southwards to view the pinnacles called the **Stacks of Duncansby** and the other very fine sea stacks and cliffs that the sea has carved out of the local sandstone.

i County Road

*Leave by the **A9** and follow it for 17 miles (27km) to Wick.*

Wick, Highland

8 Wick has been an important anchorage at least since the days of the Vikings: its name is derived from the Norse for 'bay'. Three castles testify to its strategic importance. The 12th-century castle of **Old Wick** stands to the south of the town;

SPECIAL TO...

8 *Wick, Highland* With the fishing industry and farming facing economic problems, new skills are being learned by the local people. The craftspeople of **Caithness Glass** (on the outskirts of Wick) come into this category, although their level of production is much greater than the average small-scale craft workshop. The factory has a visitor centre and tours are available.

FOR HISTORY BUFFS

Pictish brochs can be found in many places on this tour. The most substantial ones near the route are **Carn Liath** (south of Brora) and **Ousdale Broch** (north of Helmsdale). Good ones further off the route are **Dun Dornaigil** (south of Loch Hope) and **Grummore Broch** (north of Loch Naver).

SCENIC ROUTES

The superb coastal scenery, both cliffs and beaches, make this tour very attractive, especially along the north coast and near the high headlands in the northeast. The Strath of Kildonan is a fine drive for those wishing a detour.

BACK TO NATURE

The variety of good habitats, the plentiful supply of fish and the low human population have encouraged huge numbers of seabirds to nest along the coast. Particular places of interest include **Faraid Head** (near Durness) for puffins; **Duncansby Head** for many different types of cliff-nesting seabirds; **Dunnet Bay** for sea duck, divers and gulls in the winter and Golspie for sea duck and in particular, eider. **Loch Fleet** is home to many birds, especially waders, so keen birdwatchers may wish to make a detour off the **A9** and follow the southern shore of the loch before returning to Dornoch.

Laidhay Caithness Croft, Dunbeath. The main building is a thatched Caithness longhouse dating back 200 years and furnished as it would have been a century ago

further north 15th-century **Castle Girnigoe** and 17th-century **Castle Sinclair** remain as spectacular clifftop ruins.

Wick is still an important and busy place, with a fine harbour that was built for the once prosperous herring industry. An earlier harbour was built at Pulteneytown by Thomas Telford in 1806 to encourage evicted crofters to take up fishing.

Wick's **Heritage Centre**, on Bank Row, is in the middle of old buildings associated with fishing and has displays on the history of the town and the herring industry. On High Street stands Wick's old **parish church**, which has the ruined 13th-century **chapel of St Fergus** on its grounds.

ℹ️ Whitechapel Road, off High Street

*Remain on the **A9**. Turn right at a signposted unclassified road to Hill o' Many Stones.*

Hill o' Many Stones, Highland

9 This intriguing fan-shaped array of 22 rows of stones dates back to the early Bronze Age. This type of monument is unique to northern Sutherland though they are similar to ones found in Brittany. Their purpose is still an unravelled mystery though it has been postulated that this could be some sort of ancient computer that was used to predict the movement of heavenly bodies!

*Continue on the **A9** for 13 miles (21km) to Dunbeath.*

Dunbeath, Highland

10 Dunbeath is the home of the Highland writer Neil Gunn, whose books include *Sun Circle* and *Butcher's Broom*. The local **Heritage Centre** (housed in the school that Gunn attended) has displays on the lives of crofters and the history of the district.

Laidhay Caithness Croft, just north of the village, is a traditional longhouse and barn steading worked up to 1968. Parts of this thatched building may date back to the late 18th century though most of it is mid-19th-century.

*Continue on the **A9** for 16 miles (26km) to Helmsdale.*

Helmsdale, Highland

11 Set on the River Helmsdale at the seaward end of the attractive **Strath of Kildonan**, this was where some of the most infamous acts of the Clearances were carried out by Patrick Sellars on behalf of the Countess of Sutherland. The story of these sad days is admirably told in Helmsdale's **Timespan visitor centre**. This award-winning exhibition also has an exhibition on the Kildonan 'gold rush' of 1868-9. Although gold was never found in economically viable quantities, some people still go panning in the river and find small flakes of the metal.

ℹ️ Helmsdale

*Continue on the **A9** for 11 miles (18km) to Brora.*

Brora, Highland

12 Brora has the unusual distinction of having had a small coal mine based on a seam 'only' 125 million years old and, of course, a great distance from the country's main coalfields in the Midland Valley.

Today, one of its most notable industries is the **Clynelish Distillery**, Sutherland's only malt whisky distillery, and tours round it are available.

*Continue on the **A9** for 6 miles (10km) to Golspie.*

Golspie, Highland

13 This small resort lies beneath the wooded slope of **Beinn a' Bhragaidh**, near whose summit is perched a statue of the first Duke of Sutherland, who was known as the 'Leviathan of Wealth'. Between the years 1810 and 1820 he was responsible for the eviction of some 15,000 tenants from their homes, in order to use the land for lucrative sheep farming. The scars of these times are still visible all over Sutherland. Ruined croft buildings stand and decay where families were forcibly moved from their land.

A rather unusual shop in the village is the **Orcadian Stone Company**, which sells examples of rocks, minerals and fossils. It also has a fine exhibition of these natural treasures.

The Dukes of Sutherland built the nearby **Dunrobin Castle** on a site that has been fortified for many centuries. The present castle dates mainly from the 13th century but much of it was built between 1835 and 1850. Queen Victoria described it as a 'mixture of an old Scotch castle and a French chateau' and it does have a certain fairytale look about it. The gardens are extensive and contain a museum with

interesting Pictish stones, an icehouse (for storing perishable food) and an 18th-century doocot.

South of Golspie, the main road crosses the head of Loch Fleet, over a huge earthen embankment known as **The Mound**. This was constructed in 1816 by Thomas Telford, partly to support the new road heading northwards, but also to reclaim the upper reaches of the loch. Today, this section is colonised by alder and willow and has been classed as a **National Nature Reserve**. The River Fleet runs through a sluice at the end of the embankment and at certain times of the year salmon may be seen here waiting for the gate to open so they can continue their journey.

*Continue on the **A9**, then turn left at the **B9168** in order to return to Dornoch, 11 miles (17km).*

Dornoch – Tongue **59 (95)**
Tongue – Loch Eriboll **12 (19)**
Loch Eriboll – Durness **19 (31)**
Durness – Bettyhill **44 (71)**
Bettyhill – Reay **19 (31)**
Reay – Thurso **12 (19)**
Thurso – John o' Groats **20 (32)**
John o' Groats – Wick **17 (27)**
Wick – Hill o' Many Stones **10 (16)**
Hill o' Many Stones – Dunbeath **13 (21)**
Dunbeath – Helmsdale **16 (26)**
Helmsdale – Brora **11 (18)**
Brora – Golspie **6 (10)**
Golspie – Dornoch **11 (17)**

The unperturbed waters of the Golspie Burn tumble gently past the Tower Lodge Mills, passing from Loch Horn to the North Sea

FOR CHILDREN

There are a great many beautiful beaches along the coast. The ones near the east coast tend to be busier (by Highland standards) because of the number of visitors, but many on the north coast can be very quiet – and exceptionally beautiful. Well-known ones include Durness and Balnakeil.

It has to be remembered that there are fewer wet-weather facilities here than in other regions. However, there are swimming pools in Thurso and Golspie.

RECOMMENDED WALKS

Good walks include ones from Durness to Faraid Head and Duncansby Head to **Wife Geo** (a spectacular natural arch).

2 days – 107 miles (173km)

EASTER ROSS & THE BLACK ISLE

Dingwall ● Evanton ● Tain ● Portmahomack ● Fearn Abbey
Cromarty ● Rosemarkie ● Fortrose ● Dingwall

The town of Dingwall has had a chequered history, having been a Viking settlement and later a market town with the status of a royal burgh. Still an important place today, it acts as the administrative centre of Ross and Cromarty. The town's narrow streets are lined with pink sandstone buildings, but the outskirts have expanded greatly in recent years as more people have drifted towards this commercial hub. The grand *Town House* was built in 1730 and contains a small museum with displays about the area. The town is dominated by the tall tower of *Mitchell Hill*, erected in memory of Sir Hector MacDonald, a local lad who served with the Gordon Highlanders.

Burns described haggis as the 'great chieftain o' the pudden race'. It is made from sheep's heart, lungs and liver

*Leave by the **A862**. Join the **A9** heading northwards, then turn left at the **B817** to reach Evanton.*

Evanton, Highland

1 From the road, a curious monument will be seen on the summit of Cnoc Fyrish, the hill just beyond Evanton. This is a **folly** built in 1782 by General Sir Hector Munro to help alleviate local unemployment. The general had served in India and this monument is a replica of an Indian gate.

To the north of the village, the River Glass runs through a narrow glen, the narrowest part of which is known as the **Black Rock Gorge**. This intriguing cleft is 200 feet (60m) deep in some parts and only 10 feet (3m) wide. A narrow bridge over a 70-foot (20m) drop can be walked over by visitors who do not suffer from vertigo.

*Continue on the **B817** and turn left at the **B9176** (the Struie road). Turn right at **A836** and join the **A9** for Tain. Bear left at the **B9174** to enter Tain.*

Tain, Highland

2 Tain's name comes from the Norse word 'thing', meaning a parliament, as a Viking colony was established in this district. Later, the town's patron, St Duthus, was born here (in AD 1000) and he established a chapel just outside the town. After his death in Ireland his remains were brought here and interred in the 14th-century **St Duthus' Church**. The town subsequently became a place of pilgrimage and James IV often travelled here, thus increasing its prestige.

Tain's history was blotted, however, when it became an administrative centre for the Clearances. It was here that orders for the appropriation

SPECIAL TO...

The low-lying land in this part of the east coast has many good herds of dairy cattle, so look out for fresh local dairy produce. The **Highland Fine Cheeses' factory** at Tain is open to visitors wanting to discover how local cheese is made.

RECOMMENDED WALKS

The walk at Evanton to see the **Black Rock Gorge** is worthwhile. Walks to lighthouses or looking points are usually interesting: try Tarbat Ness (a circular walk from Portmahomack via the coastal path that goes past **Ballone Castle**) or the lookout at the top of the **Sutors of Cromarty**.

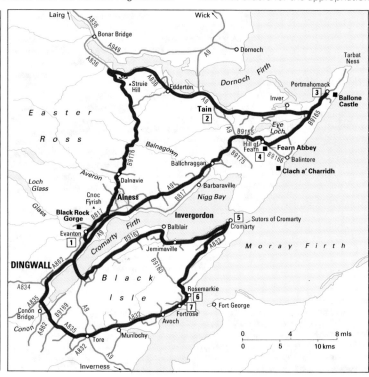

of the crofters' land were made. The deeds were carried out from the **Tolbooth** that still stands in the High Street, and it was within this building that crofters were imprisoned if they refused to obey the eviction notices. The Tolbooth is Tain's finest building; it was built between 1706 and 1733 with fine conical roofs on top of the turrets, and replaced an earlier tolbooth of 1631.

The **Glenmorangie Distillery** is renowned for its single malt whisky and the history of Tain and the surrounding area is told in the local **museum** in **Castle Brae.**

Leave by the minor road to Portmahomack. Turn left at the **B9165** *to enter the village, 10 miles (16km).*

Portmahomack, Highland

3 This pleasant lobster-fishing village sits in a broad bay with views across the Dornoch Firth. Just by the main street, an ornate Victorian cast-iron **fountain** celebrates the introduction of 'gravitation water' to the village in 1887 (water had previously come up from a well). Another unusual structure is the tower of the local **church** which is domed.

Beyond the village, a minor road leads to a **lighthouse** at **Tarbat Ness.** To the east of Portmahomack stand the ruins of **Ballone Castle** which can be reached from either the village or the lighthouse.

Return along the **B9165** *for 7 miles (11km) to Fearn Abbey.*

A beached fishing boat at Portmahomack with Dornoch Firth in the background

Fearn Abbey, Highland

4 The original **abbey** was founded in the 13th century and is unfortunately best known for the collapse of its roof in 1742, killing 42 people. This had been prophesied by the Brahan Seer, Coinneach Odhar. The 16th-century clairvoyant had the gift of the 'second sight' and during his life he gave many warnings of unhappy events that were to happen. Many of these came true and his penultimate prophecy, telling of the infidelity of the Countess of Seaforth's husband, led to him being burned alive in a barrel of tar. His last prophecy, made just before he died, foretold of the extinction of the Seaforth family. That took place in the early 19th century. Brahan, where he came from, is an estate to the southwest of Dingwall.

Continue on the **B9165** *and turn left at the* **A9.** *Cross the Cromarty Firth, then turn left at the* **B9163** *and follow it to Cromarty.*

Cromarty, Highland

5 Cromarty stands at the entrance to the Cromarty Firth, a passage dominated by the headlands of the Sutors of Cromarty and the North Sutor on the opposite shore. This is an important anchorage and was used during both world wars. Today, the firth has an oil rig fabrication site and these

FOR HISTORY BUFFS

4 *Fearn Abbey, Highland* The great Pictish cross slab, known as **Clach a' Charridh**, stands above the seaside village of **Shandwick**, near Balintore. It stands in its original position, and the face looking out to sea is engraved with a cross, angels and a beast. The other side has five panels, one of which shows a Pictish beast.

FOR CHILDREN

There are many fine beaches round the coast, including those at Cromarty, Fortrose, Portmahomack and Tain. As wet-weather alternatives, there are swimming pools in Alness, Dingwall and Tain. In addition, Alness has a sports hall and both Dingwall and Invergordon have sports centres.

BACK TO NATURE

Both the Dornoch and the Cromarty Firth are good for birdwatching, particularly for waders when the tide is out. Since the district projects some distance into the North Sea it is the first landfall for many migratory birds and **Tarbat Ness** is often a temporary resting place for visiting birds on their migratory routes. The best times of year are April and May and August to October, particularly when the winds are from the east.

SCENIC ROUTES

The sea views are particularly striking especially when driving past the firths' narrowest parts. One of the best known views is found on the Struie road; as this road descends there is a viewpoint on the right overlooking the **Kyle of Sutherland**.

Hugh Miller's cottage, Cromarty. The geologist and writer was born in the cottage in 1802. It was built by his great grandfather in the early 18th century and now houses an exhibition on Miller

massive rigs dominate the sheltered waters.

The village gained importance as it was once on the main route north from Inverness which ran along the coast and used a series of ferries across the various stretches of water. The village declined after the fishing failed and after it was decided that the railway route was to go on the other side of the firth. The most outstanding building from more prosperous times is the **Town House**, built in the 18th century. This contains the courthouse and has been opened as a visitor centre.

Cromarty's most notable inhabitant was Hugh Miller, whose **cottage** has been preserved by the National Trust for Scotland. Miller was a stonemason by trade but he never lost his childhood curiosity for collecting fossils and interesting rocks. He helped to popularise geology as he avoided the jargon of the professionals and he wrote a widely-read series of articles entitled *The Old Red Sandstone*, published in 1841. However, Miller had strong religious ideas that contradicted his scientific findings and his writings were furiously attacked by the religious bigots of the day. His thatched cottage, built in the early 18th century, contains mementoes of his life. Within the house is an example of the fossil fish named after him , *Pterichthys milleri*, and outside stands a sundial that he carved himself.

*Leave by the **A832** and follow it for 9 miles (14km) to Rosemarkie.*

Rosemarkie, Highland

6 With red sandstone houses and a red sandy beach to match, attractive Rosemarkie sits at the mouth of the Moray Firth opposite Fort George. St Moluag founded a monastic school here in the 6th century and a **Pictish stone** in the local churchyard is said to mark the saint's resting place. Other carved stones are among the exhibits in the local museum in **Groam House**, which has special displays on the Picts and the Brahan Seer.

The **Fairy Glen**, reputedly the home of a witch, runs inland from the village and there are two waterfalls further up this nicely wooded valley.

*Continue on the **A832** for 1 mile (2km) to Fortrose.*

Fortrose, Highland

7 Fortrose's main attraction is its medieval **cathedral** with an octagonal clock tower and detached Chapter House. The local bishopric was originally at Rosemarkie but moved to Fortrose early in the 13th century and the new cathedral was started then, although only completed in the 15th century. A treasure trove of over 1,000 medieval coins was found buried in the green in 1880. The harbour is well-sheltered but is now mainly used by pleasure craft.

From the village, a narrow neck of land stretches out into the Moray Firth to **Chanonry Point** where there is a lighthouse. It was here that the Brahan Seer was burned to death, and a monument has been set up to celebrate this rather remarkable man.

*Continue on the **A832** to the Tore roundabout. Join the **A835** and turn right at the **A862** to return to Dingwall, 16 miles (26km).*

Dingwall – Evanton **6 (10)**
Evanton – Tain **21 (34)**
Tain – Portmahomack **10 (16)**
Portmahomack – Fearn Abbey **7 (11)**
Fearn Abbey – Cromarty **37 (60)**
Cromarty – Rosemarkie **9 (14)**
Rosemarkie – Fortrose **1 (2)**
Fortrose – Dingwall **16 (26)**

A gushing waterfall near Sligachan, a base for exploring the Cuillin hills on the Isle of Skye

*Leave by the **A850** and follow it for 8 miles (13km) to Broadford.*

Broadford, Highland

1 This widely scattered crofting community lies beneath the **Red Hills**, a group of rounded granite mountains. This is a good base from which to explore the south of the island and is popular with walkers and other visitors.

*Continue on the **A850** for 17 miles (27km) to the Sligachan Hotel at the head of Loch Sligachan.*

Loch Sligachan, Highland

2 This is an idyllic base for any visitor, and especially for those that come to walk in the Cuillin hills. The **camp-site** by the shore must surely rate as one of Britain's finest, not for its facilities but for its position by the lochshore opposite towering 2,544-foot (775m) **Glamaig** and the view across the Inner Sound towards the mainland.

A short stroll from the road leads to an old bridge over the River Sligachan from which the Cuillin hills can be seen to greater advantage.

*Continue on the **A850** for 9 miles (14km) to Portree.*

Portree, Highland

3 This is the island's 'capital' and though the islanders might think of it as a busy place, the pace of life follows the generally relaxed Highland pattern. This is certainly a most picturesquely positioned town, with its well-sheltered harbour nestling at the foot of wooded hills.

The town's name, Port an Righ, or 'king's port', celebrates the visit here in 1540 by James V in his attempt to persuade local chiefs that they should swear allegiance to him. He brought 12 ships with him to help them make up their minds!

OVER THE SEA TO SKYE

Kyleakin ● Broadford ● Loch Sligachan ● Portree
The Storr ● Quiraing ● Kilmuir ● Uig ● Dunvegan Castle
Colbost ● Carbost ● Glen Brittle ● Torrin ● Elgol
Isleornsay ● Armadale ● Kyleakin

The 'gateway' to Skye, Kyleakin is guarded by the ruin of *Castle Moil* (or Caisteal Maol in the Gaelic), a small keep believed to have been built by the daughter of a Norse king who levied a toll on ships passing through the narrow strait of Kyle Akin. The village is busy during the summer months with visitors making the ferry crossing from Kyle of Lochalsh but the proposed bridge across the strait will certainly make changes to the traditional role of this settlement.

i Meall House (Portree)

*Leave Portree by the **A855** and continue for 7 miles (11km) to The Storr (after Loch Leathan).*

Kyleakin harbour with the ruins of Castle Moil perched on the outcrop. The castle was supposedly built by the daughter of a Norse king and commands fine views of Loch Alsh

FOR CHILDREN

The moors and lower hills of Skye provide good terrain for pony trekking and there are facilities at **Struan** (south of Dunvegan on the **A832**), **Penifiler** (south of Portree) and **Uig**. However, it must be remembered that Skye's weather can be very mixed.

FOR HISTORY BUFFS

3 *Portree, Highland* South of Portree, the **B883** road leads to the settlement of **Braes**, where a monument celebrates the battles between local crofters and the police in 1882. The locals had asked their Laird, Lord MacDonald, for extra land on which to graze their animals. He refused, even though the crofters were prepared to pay, and they decided to withhold their rents. Court orders were then taken out against them but the orders were seized and torn up when the sheriff's officers tried to deliver them. In a further confrontation, the local police were helped by 50 policemen from Glasgow (and backed up by naval ships standing by with troops aboard should the 'trouble' spread!). These events caused a public outcry about the way in which landowners treated crofters and this led to legislation being passed which guaranteed fair rents and security of tenure.

The Storr, Highland

4 As the road heads northwards it runs beneath a steep escarpment, the highest point of which is The Storr, 2,363 feet (719m) high. To the right of this can be seen the tall pinnacle called the **Old Man of Storr** which is 160 feet (49m) tall. This is the site of Britain's most spectacular example of landslipping; the great jumble of boulders, screes and pinnacles indicates where huge chunks of the mountainside have slipped as the weak underlying clays and limestones collapsed under the weight of the overlying lavas.

*Continue on the **A855** for 12 miles (19km) to the Quiraing.*

Quiraing, Highland

5 To the northwest of the crofting community of **Staffin**, another escarpment indicates the site of a massive landslip. This is known as the Quiraing and is best approached on foot from the Staffin to Uig road. Nature has produced some strange shapes here, and some of the features have been given names like the Table, the Prison and the Needle.

*Continue on the **A855** for 13 miles (21km) to Kilmuir.*

Kilmuir, Highland

6 This scattered crofting community is home to the **Skye Museum of Island Life** which has a number of attractive thatched cottages that have been restored to show how people lived in these small houses a century ago.

Nearby, a tall **monument** in the local graveyard marks the grave of Flora MacDonald. She has a very special place in Scots history as the woman who helped Bonnie Prince Charlie escape after Culloden. He had fled to South Uist but found the island crawling with hundreds of government soldiers, all of them keen to capture a man with a price of £30,000 on his head. Flora disguised the prince as her maidservant Betty Burke

Magnificent Dunvegan Castle, part of which dates back to the 10th century

and smuggled him over to Skye, from where he reached the mainland and escaped to France.

To the north of Kilmuir stand the ruins of **Duntulm Castle**, built in the early 17th century by the MacDonalds to strengthen their position against their rivals, the MacLeods. The building stands on a crag, protected by cliffs and steep slopes on the three seaward sides and a dry ditch on the landward side.

*Continue on the **A855** for 6 miles (10km) to Uig.*

Uig, Highland

7 This little port is the terminus for the ferries that serve Lochmaddy on North Uist and Tarbert on Harris, so the harbourside can be busy around sailing times. A little **tower** overlooks the harbour and though it looks rather old, it is in fact a Victorian folly dating back to the 19th century.

*Leave by the **A856** and turn right when the **A850** is met. Follow this to Dunvegan Castle.*

Dunvegan Castle, Highland

8 The home of the chiefs of the Clan MacLeod was built as a keep in the 14th century with its only entrance through the sea gate. Within the castle is the famous 'fairy flag', said to have been given to a MacLeod chief by a fairy. The flag is of Eastern origin and the legend is that it will protect the clan if waved at moments of great danger. Also on display is the drinking horn owned by the chieftain Sir Rory Mor: this can hold the equivalent of two bottles of wine, and it is claimed that he could drain it in one draught!

On the other side of Loch Dunvegan stand the two flat-topped hills called **MacLeod's Tables**. Their name recalls a chieftain bragging to a Lowlander of the size of his dining table; to prove his boast he entertained his guest on one of the summits.

*Leave by the **A863**, then turn right at the **B884** to Colbost.*

Colbost, Highland

9 There is a little **folk museum** here with a thatched cottage and a display of 19th-century furniture and farming implements. If you have never smelled a peat fire burning then here is your chance!

*Return along the **B884** and turn right at the **A863**. Turn right at the **B8009** and follow this to Carbost.*

Carbost, Highland

10 This is the site of Skye's only distillery, the **Talisker Distillery**. The peat used to dry the grain gives the whisky its distinctive flavour.

*Return along the **B8009** and turn right at the minor road that leads down Glen Brittle, 9 miles (14km).*

Glen Brittle, Highland

11 Most visitors to Skye will have heard of the Cuillin hills, the serrated ridges of which provide marvellous hillwalking. Many of the hills' lower slopes are covered with loose scree, while many of the upper parts are bare rock with little or no vegetation on them, and these are the

preserve of experienced hillwalkers. For walkers trying to capture all the 'Munros' (Scottish hills with a peak over 3,000 feet (914m) high), their most difficult obstacle is usually the **Inaccessible Pinnacle** on **Sgurr Dearg** which involves climbing a pinnacle at the top of the mountain. Definitely not for casual walkers.

The foot of the glen is often busy with walkers and climbers who are here to scale the hills. Looking up and around, there are marvellous views of

A fluted basalt pillar rising out from the Quiraing rock pinnacles

the jagged hills with their long steep scree slopes.

*Return to the **B8009** and turn right. Turn right at the **A863** and continue to Sligachan, then turn right at the **A850**. Follow this to Broadford, then turn right at the **A881** in order to reach Torrin, 36 miles (58km).*

BACK TO NATURE

8 *Dunvegan Castle, Highland* Common seals and great grey Atlantic seals are found in Loch Dunvegan and boat trips to the seal colonies are available from Dunvegan. Golden eagles and white-tailed sea eagles may also be seen in the locality. The latter are the subject of a reintroduction programme in Scotland.

In spring, the flower-rich meadows can be a colourful sight and alpine species are sometimes found growing beside the road in upland areas.

SCENIC ROUTES

In good weather the whole of this tour passes through scenery which is truly memorable. Perhaps the most dramatic parts are north of Portree when the **Old Man of Storr** is seen with **Loch Fada** in the foreground, and also going down **Glen Brittle** and seeing the massive northern corries of the **Cuillin hills**.

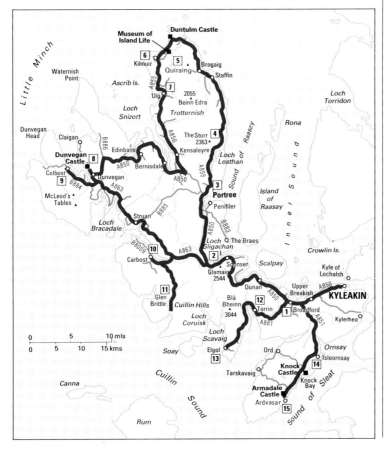

RECOMMENDED WALKS

Skye offers countless opportunities for walking – provided the weather is kind!

One straightforward walk starts at **Claigan**, which is north of Dunvegan. This follows the shore and leads to a little coral beach.

The **Old Man of Storr** can be reached from a roadside path but the path is steep and there is a lot of loose scree in places. However, the landscape here is quite unique and the view is a fine reward indeed.

The **Cuillin hills** should certainly not be attempted by walkers with little hillwalking experience, but there are low-level walks that are easier. The best advice is to buy one of the local walking guides which are available.

SPECIAL TO . . .

Crabs are often landed by fishing boats at small jetties (for example at Elgol) or just on a suitable beach, so keep a lookout for local boats coming inshore. Many of the small boats make special deliveries to local hotels once they have landed their catch, so the food could hardly be fresher.

Many people on Skye speak Gaelic and road signs and other notices are written in English and Gaelic.

Perhaps the finest scenery on the island, the Cuillin hills seen from above Loch Scavaig near the crofting village of Elgol. Many of the peaks soar to over 3,000 feet (915m)

Torrin, Highland

12 Torrin is best known for its fine view of the 3,044-foot (928m) mountain, **Blà Bheinn** (or Blaven) and its precipitous rocky ridge known as Clach Glas. The latter entices the experienced climber. A couple of quarries near by are sources of the white Skye marble.

*Continue on the **A881** and follow it for 10 miles (16km) to Elgol.*

Elgol, Highland

13 Elgol, a tiny collection of houses overlooking Loch Scavaig, has a small jetty from which there is one of the best views of the Cuillin hills. From here it is possible to appreciate the shape of the complex, with a ring of hills surrounding Loch Coruisk. Boat trips to Loch Coruisk are available.

Looking in the other direction, the view over the sea encompasses the islands of Soay, Rum, Canna and Eigg.

*Return along the **A881** to Broadford, then turn right at the **A850**. Turn right again at the **A851** to Isleornsay.*

Isleornsay, Highland

14 The village lies a little off the main road. At the road end is a headland on which there is an inn, a pier and a view towards the tidal island of Ornsay. The wilderness of Knoydart stands opposite, on the other side of the Sound of Sleat.

Further south lies **Knock Bay** and above this is a rocky mound on which stands **Knock Castle**. These ivy-covered ruins are sometimes called Castle Camus. It was built in medieval times by the MacDonalds of Sleat and

its best known occupant was a lady known as Mary of the Castle.

*Continue on the **A851** for 8 miles (13km) to Armadale.*

Armadale, Highland

15 Armadale can be a busy little place at times as it has a car ferry connection with Mallaig, but it is really a very picturesque spot in a sheltered bay.

Close to the village stands the **Clan Donald Centre**. This is in the grounds of the now partly ruined **Armadale Castle**, which was built in 1815, and has displays on the history of the MacDonalds. There are also gardens and woodland trails in the grounds.

This part of Skye, known as Sleat, is sometimes called the 'Garden of Skye' because of its luxuriant coastal vegetation. Dr Johnson visited Armadale in 1773 and was duly impressed by what he saw of the fine gardens here, commenting that the planting of the gardens 'proved that the present nakedness of the Hebrides is not wholly the fault of Nature'.

An alternative route back to Isleornsay (instead of taking the A851) is via Tarskavaig on the western side of Sleat. This route gives really superb views over to Elgol and Rum. There are also fine unspoiled beaches at Tarskavaig Bay and Ord.

*Return along the **A851** towards Broadford. Turn right at the **A850** to return to Kyleakin, 24 miles (39km).*

A silver cross of Celtic design in Iona's abbey buildings

ℹ️ Main Street

*Leave by the **A848** to Salen, then continue along the coast on the **A849** to Craignure.*

Craignure, Strathclyde

1 This is the island's main ferry terminal and the first place in Mull that most visitors will see. **Torosay Castle** stands close to Craignure and visitors can reach the castle by driving further down the road, strolling along a forest walk from Craignure or taking a trip on the local miniature railway. The castle is not a fortified structure at all, but a Victorian mansion built in 1856; it has extensive gardens designed by Sir Robert Lorimer and a 'statue garden' with 19 Italian figures.

A little further down the coast stands the stronghold **Duart Castle**. This was originally built in the 13th century by the MacDougalls but later passed into the hands of the Mac-Leans. Much of the present structure belongs to their 14th-century additions.

*Take the **A849** to Strathcoil, then turn left at the unclassified road to Lochbuie, 14 miles (23km).*

Lochbuie, Strathclyde

2 The minor road down to Lochbuie is narrow and winding and passes through a well-wooded glen and a landscape that is quite different from the open moorlands so common in much of Mull. At the shore, the wide bay is ringed by hills and to the east stands the ruined tower of **Moy Castle**, a Maclaine castle of the 15th century. This ivy-covered castle has a special dungeon off the dining room. It is a pit filled with water to a depth of 9 feet (3m) with a stone sticking up in the middle of the pool; this is where the poor prisoner sat – in total darkness!

The fertile land at the head of the loch earned the local estate the name the 'Garden of Mull'. Behind **Lochbuie House** stands a reminder of

SPANISH GOLD & CELTIC CROSSES

Tobermory ● Craignure ● Lochbuie ● Iona ● Gruline
Kilninian ● Calgary Bay ● Dervaig ● Tobermory

Mull's 'capital', Tobermory, can be a busy place with Main Street thronged with cars, caravans, local shoppers and lots of visitors strolling about. This is probably the best-sheltered bay on the west coast and it is usually full of small pleasure boats; large ocean-going yachts can also be seen in the harbour. The most celebrated ship to visit Tobermory was the *San Juan de Sicilia*, a galleon belonging to the Spanish Armada. It survived the naval battle with Drake in 1588 only to sink in the bay, not too far from the shore. Many people have attempted to recover items from the wreck, urged on by stories that the ship carried gold.

The *Mull Museum* on Main Street has displays on local history, the island's social history and the story of the Spanish galleon which belongs to the Duke of Argyll, and a visit to this excellent little museum gives a most interesting introduction to the island and its people.

Tobermory's *Leedaig Whisky Distillery*, built in 1822, has a visitor centre and tours round the premises.

The Scottish baronial architecture of Torosay Castle complemented by its splendid setting. Much of this Victorian mansion and its Italian terraced gardens is open to the public

FOR CHILDREN

There are a number of good beaches round the coast, notably at Calgary Bay, which is ideal for bathing, and Lochbuie. The **narrow gauge railway at Torosay Castle** is always appealing to children (and adults!). This is the country's only island railway and was originally built in 1984 to encourage reluctant walkers to go from Craignure Pier to Torosay Castle; however, it has become an attraction in its own right. It has four engines, two of them steam-powered.

SPECIAL TO ...

As well as having its own whisky distillery, the island can also boast a very delicious liqueur, '**Columba Cream**' (a mix of whisky, cream and honey) and two vermouths, '**The Mull Riveter**' and the '**Isle of Mull Vermouth**'.

BACK TO NATURE

Much of Mull has been built up by basalt lavaflows from long-lost volcanoes and the island has some unique volcanic features that are worth seeing. The uninhabited peninsula on the northern side of Loch Scridain is aptly-named '**The Wilderness**' and on its southern shore is the world-famous **McCulloch's Fossil Tree**, a large conifer that was engulfed by lava. It can only be approached at low tide and then after a long walk, so careful preparation is needed for a visit.

Another widely known place is the island of **Staffa**, where **Fingal's Cave** provided the inspiration for Mendelssohn's famous overture.

Compared to many islands off the west coast, Mull has considerable areas of native woodland as well as plantations. Look for woodland birds here, while golden eagles and buzzards prefer rocky crags. Offshore, seabirds, including guillemots, can be seen while others feed unobtrusively along the shoreline.

SCENIC ROUTES

Most of the coastal roads give fine views over the sea, especially the sections by **Loch na Keal** and **Loch Tuath** where there are excellent views of the offshore islands, the largest of which is **Ulva**, where the parents of Scots missionary, David Livingstone, came from.

a very early settlement, a **stone circle** with nine uprights and three outlying monoliths.

*Return to the **A849** and turn left. Follow this road to Fionnphort and take the ferry over to Iona. Cars should be left at Fionnphort.*

Iona, Strathclyde

3 The small island of Iona is a magnet for summer visitors, and is a place of great historic and spiritual significance. Part of Scotland's history is re-created in its **abbey**, now painstakingly reconstructed using traditional materials.

The historic importance of Iona stems from the arrival here in AD563 of the Irish missionary Columba who established a monastery. The island became a religious centre and its influence spread throughout Scotland and into England, but it suffered at the hands of the Viking raiders in the 8th century. A Benedictine abbey was founded around the start of the 13th century and the oldest part of the abbey dates from that time. At the Reformation, there were over 300 crosses standing near the abbey but many were broken during those turbulent times and only a few massive ones remain as beautifully carved memorials to the skills of the early craftsmen.

Apart from the abbey, there are a number of other buildings worth looking at, including the ruined **Augustinian nunnery** and **St Oran's Chapel**. The chapel is the oldest building on Iona. The story behind its name involves its troubled construction. The walls kept collapsing and to placate the evil spirit that was felt to be causing this problem, it was

decided that a human sacrifice was needed to be placed under the foundations – Oran was the volunteer. The chapel is in the **Reilig Oran** – the graveyard of kings – where many of Scotland's early kings and queens, and a number of Irish, Norwegian and possibly French kings are buried.

*Return to Fionnphort and follow the **A849** eastwards., Turn left at the **B8035** in order to reach Gruline.*

Gruline, Strathclyde

4 At Gruline, a narrow road (right) leads to the **mausoleum** of Major-General Lachlan Macquarrie. Born locally, after a career in the British army he became Governor-General of New South Wales in Australia, a post he held from 1810 to 1820. In recognition of this connection, the building is maintained on behalf of the National Trust of Australia.

*Continue on the **B8035**, then turn left on to the **B8073** to reach Kilninian, 13 miles (21km).*

Kilninian, Strathclyde

5 This little **church** overlooking the sea dates back to at least 1561 but the present structure was built in 1755. At the back of the church there are a number of large carved grave slabs from the early 16th century.

Dun Aisgain is found a little further along the road, standing on a rocky knoll overlooking the sea. This defensive site still has some of its 6-feet (2m) thick walls intact, part of which has traces of the internal mural gallery that was built within it. The dun is best approached from Burg.

*Continue on the **B8073** for 7 miles (11km) to Calgary Bay.*

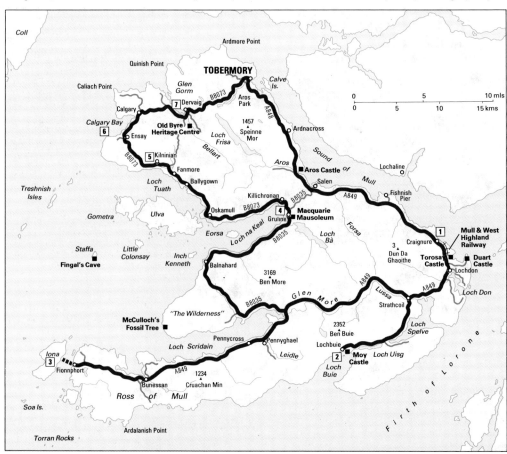

Calgary Bay, Strathclyde

6 This wide bay with its sandy beach is a popular stopping place for visitors. Few people live here now, but on the northern side of the bay there are deserted townships and an old pier. The builders of the pier took full advantage of the local geology when they used a prominent volcanic dyke as one of the walls. The existence of this prominent vertical sheet of rock could have led to the name of the bay, as Calgary may have come from the Gaelic word Calagharaidh, meaning 'the haven by the wall'.

The town of Calgary in Alberta, Canada, was named after the bay.

*Continue on the **B8073** for 6 miles (10km) to Dervaig.*

Dervaig, Strathclyde

7 Dervaig is a very pleasant little community that was established as a 'planned village' in 1799. The village and its environs have been designated a conservation area and this is a good base from which to explore the north of the island.

The narrow Gribun Pass wedged between the waters of Loch na Keal and a dramatically abrupt cliff backdrop; the loch's Celtic name translates to 'Loch of the Cliffs'

The most obvious village landmark is the church's **round tower**, reminiscent of Irish churches. The building is relatively modern, having been constructed as recently as 1905.

Two other local places of interest are the **Mull Little Theatre** and, a little further out of the village, the **Old Byre Heritage Centre**, which illustrates crofting life.

*Continue on the **B8073** and return to Tobermory, 6 miles (10km).*

Tobermory – Craignure	**21 (33)**
Craignure – Lochbuie	**14 (23)**
Lochbuie – Iona	**39 (63)**
Iona – Gruline	**37 (60)**
Gruline – Kilninian	**13 (21)**
Kilninian – Calgary Bay	**7 (11)**
Calgary Bay – Dervaig	**6 (10)**
Dervaig – Tobermory	**6 (10)**

FOR HISTORY BUFFS

Tobermory, Strathclyde Just north of Salen stands the ruined tower of **Aros Castle**. Like **Duart Castle** further down the coast, this commands a fine view over the Sound of Mull and was an important bastion of the power of the Lords of the Isles, the rulers of this region of Scotland from the 14th to the 16th centuries.

RECOMMENDED WALKS

There are marked forest walks at places such as **Aros Park** (south of Tobermory) and **Glen Gorm** (north of Dervaig). Iona is well-endowed with tracks and paths and it has many interesting places to see (such as the old marble quarry) well away from the abbey and the throng of visitors.

INDEX

References to captions are in *italic.*

ACKNOWLEDGEMENTS

The Automobile Association would like to thank the following photographers and libraries for their help in the preparation of this book.

D HARDLEY 9 Sweetheart Abbey.

INTERNATIONAL PHOTOBANK Cover Eilean Donan Castle.

SPECTRUM COLOUR LIBRARY 20 Kirkcudbright Harbour, 33 Jedburgh Abbey, 34 Etterick Water.

All remaining photographs are held in the Association's own library (AA PHOTO LIBRARY) with contributions from: M Adelman, J Beazley, J Carnie, D Corrance, S Gibson Pictures, D Hardley, A J Hopkins, S & O Mathews, P Sharpe, M Taylor, R Weir, H Williams.